Ed Hor
Money .

should have on hand for easy access and correct commu-
nication about receiving an offering. After years
and years of receiving tithes and offerings, you find
yourself repeating the same thing over and over again.
The worst part of this process is that people become
dull of hearing because they have heard it all before
and end up completely unmotivated to give at all or
especially above their normal giving. This book will
help you to have a fresh insight into words that will
help motivate the congregation to be the very best givers they can be every week. We all know how important it is for people to remain faithful in their giving.
Good job, Ed Horak! This is a very timely book in
these economic conditions.

—Pastor Jim Cobrae, Senior Pastor,
The Rock Church and World Outreach Center,
San Bernardino, California, USA

Ed manages to thaw the indifference many leaders
have towards the frosty subject of money with boldness
and clarity. *The Money Moment* lays a biblical foundation of how the individual and church should steward
God's resources, particularly finances. He highlights
the crisis facing the church if we ignore the truth God
has so clearly laid out in his Word regarding financial
stewardship. The timing of this book could not be bet-

ter, and I believe this it is a prophetically inspired for the time we are living in with the current global economic crisis. I am convinced that God is speaking to the church about how we handle our finances so that we may be delivered through bad economic times, and glorify him in the process. Ed gives a practical plan of how to take our churches to a higher understanding of good stewardship by introducing the "money moment." These biblical truths on stewardship (handling tithes and offerings) can be shared with the congregation on a weekly basis for one year. The work of preparing an offering message is simplified when using his book. I highly recommend this book to every leader that wants to see financial growth as well as spiritual in their church and also to every believer who wants to understand financial stewardship on a balanced basis.

—Pastor Tom Inglis, President, Psalmody International,
Senior Pastor, Sydney Life Church,
Sydney, Australia

I was very pleased to read Ed Horak's book, *The Money Moment*. He has provided a great service to pastors and leaders who have the responsibility of teaching God's people about giving and has created a great tool that I believe will be very beneficial. Ed's practical and biblical teaching reminds us that the receiving of tithes and offerings is not merely a means of getting money for the church, but is indeed a valid and important part of the worship experience for believers. As such, it deserves thoughtful preparation; the offering should not just be an afterthought. *The Money Moment* will further help pastors by providing seed thoughts for actual offerings. This is a resource that will prove to be a valuable addition to the libraries of ministers.

—Pastor Tony Cooke, President,
Tony Cooke Ministries,
Broken Arrow, Oklahoma, USA

THE
MONEY
MOMENT

THE
MONEY
MOMENT

How to Encourage a Lifestyle of Giving

Edmund Horak

TATE PUBLISHING & *Enterprises*

Published by Tate Publishing & Enterprises, LLC
127 E. Trade Center Terrace | Mustang, Oklahoma 73064 USA
1.888.361.9473 | www.tatepublishing.com

Tate Publishing is committed to excellence in the publishing industry. The company reflects the philosophy established by the founders, based on Psalm 68:11,
"The Lord gave the word and great was the company of those who published it."

Book design copyright © 2010 by Tate Publishing, LLC. All rights reserved.
Cover design by Tyler Evans, Janine Horak & Nathan Coonrod
Interior design by Lindsay B. Behrens

Published in the United States of America

ISBN: 978-1-61566-647-8
Religion / Christian Life / Stewardship & Giving
09.12.29

TABLE OF CONTENTS

HOW TO USE
THIS BOOK

The Money Moment' is primarily designed to equip Christian leaders on how to encourage a lifestyle of giving in their own lives, ministries, and churches. Leaders set the 'financial tone' amongst their followers, and the success of any fund raising depends on the leader's integrity, transparency, trust and the methods they adopt. Pastors, ministers, lay leaders, board members, department heads, and financial officers will all benefit from the practical insights contained in *The Money Moment.* This resource will give you the tools you can use on a weekly basis to raise the level of giving in your ministry and church. Churches that have used this systematic approach have noticed an increase first in the congregation's understanding of God's financial plan and second a measurable increase in the level of tithes and offerings.

In addition, the weekly 'Money Moments' may serve as an encouraging devotional for anyone interested in what God has to say on the subject of finances. Faith will arise as the Word on financial stewardship is heard, read and meditated on (Joshua 1:8).

The book begins in Section A with some crucial pointers about how to encourage a lifestyle of giving; followed by important practicalities in Section B, and then in Section C and D provides a ready reference for the weekly receiving of tithes and offerings. Section E gives useful resource material that could be used in any stewardship teaching series to equip the congregation with a solid scriptural foundation for a fruitful lifestyle of giving. Section F looks on the lighter side of things as it is often useful to laugh together at ourselves over money matters.

The Money Moment does not cover special capital fund raising campaigns for church buildings and facilities. These are too specific to be covered in this book, so the focus remains on the weekly opportunity leaders get in exhorting their followers in the essentials of responsible giving.

This useful reference will not only expose you to an enriching variety of money matter topics, but it will also sharpen your own ministry 'sword' (Isaiah 49:2) so that you can more effectively encourage God's people in financially supporting the spread of the gospel.

SECTION A

How to Encourage Giving

Introduction

It takes more than just good preaching and prayer to spread the gospel in the world. The gospel may still be free, but the channels through which it flows are not. Have you tried to build a church building lately, or go on radio or TV to spread the message? Did you ever notice that in the great outpouring of the Holy Spirit at Pentecost and beyond in Jerusalem, there was a parallel outpouring of giving to finance the gospel? Talk about prosperity with a purpose or money with a mission; they had it all and then some. They sold houses and pooled their hard-earned resources to establish God's kingdom. Today however, things are a little different in most of the church world. May this book help you and your ministry be a significant part of the solution.

The Challenge

Most ministers love to teach sermon subjects like how to pray, witness, evangelize, worship, walk in love, grow spiritually in God, and so on. However, there is a vital need to also teach on matters of financial stewardship in some detail. In America, the savings rate is at it the lowest level in sixty years, and personal consumer debt and inflation often exceeds any increase in income. It is estimated that 40 percent of church members in the USA pay more than $2000 per year in short term debt interest, not including their mortgage interest. Not surprisingly almost a third of 'born again' Christians say it is impossible to 'get ahead' because of financial debt they have incurred. Consumer debt in the United States has increased an average of 8 percent annually over the last 20 years since 1985, with the average family now carrying $58,500 in debt.

Gambling is a problem even in many Christian families, and unfortunately the divorce rate among Christian marriages is up. This has an impact on a family's finances; and most resultant single-parent households struggle financially to make ends meet. More people declare bankruptcy each year than graduate from all colleges and universities. In 1990, one in three hundred households declared bankruptcy annually. In 2001, it was one in sixty-nine! Historically, According to the Unites States Department of Justice, bankruptcy filings have grown overall from about 110,000 in 1960, to over 1.6 million in 2003. In 2008 as many as 1,416,902 people in the United States filed for either personal or business bankruptcy. 91 percent of bankruptcy filers have suffered a job loss, medical event or divorce, and the average age of filers is 38.

It could be argued that society as a whole is under 'stress' at worst, and 'misguided' at best, what with the same amount of money being spent on household pets as on support of all church ministries put together: $40 Billion annually in the USA alone! Still more ($60 billion per annum) is spent on weight loss programs and products for overweight individuals. Church budgets are typically planned on a giving rate per congregant of 2–3 percent of their incomes. Worldwide, Christians are estimated to have an income totaling $16 Trillion, yet in 2007 only an estimated 2 percent, or $370 Billion, was donated to Christian causes: church and Para–Church organizations put together.

Many churches and ministries face increasing financial pressure. Tithing has decreased almost every year for the past three decades. Today, the average Christian household gives only 2.5 percent of their income to the work of the Lord and 1.7 percent to other charitable organizations. These percentages are lower than during the Great Depression! It is estimated that the average American churchgoer gives only twenty dollars annually to foreign missions. Contrast this with an average of $1,174 per year spent on gambling across the whole population.

Christians generally have not been adequately trained to handle their finances according to the Word. It may be because ministers have not been trained themselves! Only 2–4 percent of Seminaries and Christian Colleges teach financial stewardship as part of their curriculum. Then 80 percent of pastors have no books on Christian Stewardship in their libraries, and are thus assumed to have little or no formal training in this key area to adequately lead their congregations. Sadly 60 percent of candidates for marriage counseling identify money matters as a major problem in their marriages. Pastors and other Christian leaders with money problems themselves find it difficult to counsel their own congregants in this vital area. Many turn to Para–Church financial professionals for help—not a bad idea in the current state of things. Yet it is God's best for the local church to be a center of wisdom for prospering in all areas of life.

When giving is viewed across the generations, the next generation is found to be less generous than their parents or the previous generation. People who are not taught to give philanthropically in their youth are less likely to grow up with a generous heart. Statistically, the middle class baby boomers in America (who earn between $40 000 and $100 000 per annum) give less percentage wise today, than the lower class (those earning less than $20 000 per annum). Then, in many churches, the sixty–five–year–old–plus group contributes the lion's share of most church operating budgets.

Not only are the financial consequences for continuing church ministry quite severe, but so are the spiritual consequences. How a Christian handles his/her money is directly related to his/her spiritual growth. Jesus teaches that only when we steward the resources given to us properly can we enjoy the reward of true riches: a vital fruitful relationship with Him (Matthew 25:21 and Luke 16:11). Only when Christians are challenged and taught to submit their finances to Christ will the competition for their souls be settled. Money and Christ cannot both be served at the same time. Money must be our servant, not our master. Our consumer–based society conditions even unsuspecting Christians into a mind–set of indulgence and selfishness at the expense of responsible living that leaves enough time, energy, and will to help the less fortunate through genuine church ministry outreach. We only genuinely prosper to the degree our souls prosper.

All discipleship training should have financial stewardship built in, and for God's ministers to neglect this vital area is as bad as neglecting to teach someone on prayer, worship, and missions. Ways should be found to train all generations including the little children in God's Word concerning stewardship. This must be a dual responsibility between church and parents. There are over two thousand verses in the Bible that deal with material matters. Jesus even dedicated two–thirds of His parables to the subject of money and possessions; it was that important to Him. It must become that important to us as well. We are under command to preach and teach all that He commanded the disciples (Matthew 28:20). That surely includes the weighting He put on the subject of material things compared to other topics.

On an encouraging note, although giving in the modern American church falls far short of God's minimum standard of the tithe, American Christians fund up to ninety percent of all missions and outreaches worldwide! To see ministries that reach out to feed the world's poor, build and staff medical missions, rescue young children from human trafficking, build orphanages, dig water wells and send disaster recovery teams to areas hit by nature's wrath is inspiring. Churches across the world are increasingly standing up to meet the needs of helpless others in Africa, Asia, the Middle East and South America. They are leading the way compassionately building sustainable relief and restoration projects in the agricultural, educational and medical fields.

Yet, imagine what more could be done if the percentages were to rise by just 7 percent above the current rates to a full tithe or 10 percent worldwide. Of course, throwing money at the problem is not always the solution, but if it can be matched with a heart of commitment, wisdom and sustainability—more efficient outreach—there is no limit to what God can do through His people in the years to come. It is His heart to reach mankind with hands of compassion: yours and mine.

You and Your Church or Ministry

Are you living in the financial land of not enough, just enough, or more than enough? This resource will prayerfully help you create a culture of giving in your church. That's right; you as the leader have to create a new mind–set in your church. No one else will. That's the way it works. Leaders lead from the front, not the back. Obviously you must be convinced that God delights in your well–being and will supply not only your needs but also the desires and dreams you have to reach your community for Christ. Our focus in this book will be more on the practicalities of creating a new culture of giving in the church than on trying to convince you that God wants you to enjoy and steward His abundance wisely.

I was born again into a church community where giving as a lifestyle was actively taught and modeled. For many, generous acts became almost as natural as breathing. So the hang–ups I had to overcome were from my own family background and not some set of unbiblical death–dealing church traditions. Now if you come from such a background, hold on to your seat, take a deep breath, and trust God to sort things out for you. He is big enough, after all, to teach us all a thing or two about His financial plan. If you are from a part of the world other than so–called first world nations, remember that God (Jesus) was from the Middle East. Prosperity, giving, and stewardship are not modern Western inventions, but have been around for a long time. Remember that the earth was created to minister to Adam, and Adam was created to minister to God. All the wealth and the resources this earth has to offer are owned by God, but stewarded or managed by man. So let's get equipped, worship God, and get the job done of reaching the world for Jesus using any and all means we can get our hands on.

Develop a Culture of Giving

Have you ever seen very young children naturally share their toys? Probably not. They have to be taught to share and be generous. Likewise in a church, a number of steps must be taken to counter the unrenewed, naturally selfish tendency of many immature Christians. It takes <u>faith, commitment, and trust to be a giver.</u> As we have seen, it is estimated that most churches' level of tithing commitment among regular members and attendees is below ten percent. That means that ninety percent of your people are either ignorant or indifferent, or simply disobedient to God's command to support His work. Your people's commitment to support the gospel follows the conviction of the Holy Spirit as the Word is preached on giving.

Consider the following outline that you could use to develop a culture of giving in your church. Remember it is not going to happen by mere wishful thinking or by some sort of vague spiritual osmosis. You have to be seen to be leading in this matter and speaking the Word so that faith for giving can arise as your people hear what God has to say about their finances.

Establish Bible Reasons for Giving

Begin by establishing Bible reasons for a lifestyle of giving. Show that giving to a ministry is not merely about keeping the ministry afloat or the bills and salaries paid. This may be obvious to most, but emphasize the fact that financing the greatest adventure given to man—to preach the gospel to the ends of the earth—is a great privilege, and that God expects us to joyfully participate in, and favor His righteous cause.

The gospel of forgiveness may be free for all to receive, but it costs to get it out. Even Jesus relied on the substance of His supporters to facilitate his ministry. Women of substance and many others gave of their best to support the preaching of the gospel (Luke 8:3). Jesus spoke more on practical money matters than any other subject: the parable of the talents (Matthew 25:15–28); the widow's two mites (Mark 12:41–44); the priority of seeking God's kingdom (Matthew 6:33), to list just three examples. In the Jewish mind–set, there was no artificial separation between a person's spiritual walk and their finances. In fact, how you conducted yourself in the natural affairs of life indicated the state of your heart. The spirit, soul and body were all connected. That's why the Apostle John could pray: 'Beloved, I pray that you may prosper in all things and be in health, just as your soul prospers' (3 John 2).

Eliminate Excuses, Your Own and in Your Church

Tackle those excuses. Not all giving problems are rooted in the congregation's ignorance or indifference about giving. Sometimes we have to begin by eliminating the embarrassment about raising funds for the work of the ministry in the leadership of a church or ministry. True, some will always say that preachers and pastors are always looking for a handout. That's their problem for opting out of their God–required responsibility to support the gospel. Maybe some preachers are focused on just that, but the majority are not. They are sincere about their call and ministry, but nevertheless often awkward about money matters from behind the pulpit. They come up with all sorts of ways of almost apologetically slipping in offering time 'under the radar', so to speak. They hardly ever talk about it, and when they do, it's not with bold authority, as if they have a problem with money.

If the preacher is not free, how can the congregation be free? Be like Jesus, who never seemed to have a problem about receiving contributions from rich and poor alike, even talking at length about giving and all its associated heart matters. Whom the 'Son sets free' in money matters is 'free indeed' in money matters (John 8:36). Don't be held hostage to fear or intimidation. Others will think what they will, but only what God thinks, is really what counts. If people think you are just after their money, they have the problem, not you. You are free. So live free from the fear of man and do what God called you to do. He will back you up as you stand with integrity.

Some of you might say, 'Brother Big Bucks will be offended'. Wealthy congregants also need their minds renewed to God's ways (1 Timothy 6:17–19) just like anyone else. Equip them with the Word and give them a chance to renew their minds and go forward in God in this crucial area of giving. Put your trust in God to supply your needs, not man. The fear of man traps you into low–level living. God must be in control, not any man or any church board for that matter. Yes, they can and should provide godly counsel and serve in matters of accountability, but are never to come before God's plan and vision.

Set the tone in your church and ministry. Create a respect for this part of the gospel. Tithes, offerings, and practical support of the gospel are holy things. Whatever we touch ought to be sanctified. Let God work on your heart and settle some things about finances. Then launch out with boldness. After all, the righteous one is bold as a lion. Deal with any questionable stuff in the handling of finances, personal and church related. When your conscience is clear before God, you can roar like a lion and scatter the enemy.

When you give a clear exposition of God's requirements and promises, you eliminate excuses in the congregation. The average person will be tempted to hide behind their favorite excuses in order to avoid committed and consistent giving. Hold your people accountable to the Word. Although everyone must individually give an account to God for his or her own stewardship, leaders will undergo stricter judgment for whether they have equipped and challenged their people even in this matter of financial stewardship.

Some people simply do not know what God expects of them with their finances. They are untaught and ignorant, and your job is to teach or equip them with God's Word (Ephesians 4:11–12). Then there are those who are either indifferent because of their spiritual dullness or plain selfish disobedience. Either way, they have to be challenged to change through prayer and ministry of the Word. For years, I have used several Scriptures to pray for God's people to walk in financial freedom with a spirit of generosity. God's will and kingdom is fulfilled on earth when we pray and obey. It does not come by simply wishing and hoping on the one hand, and complaining on the other. God has His ways, and they must be implemented for things to function the way He intended them.

Expose the Vision

Expose the church's vision to your people on a regular basis. People are more likely to support vision than appeals to meet some budgetary deficit. Some church leaders have found that people need to be reminded of the cardinal elements of their church's vision at least once every six weeks. You cannot assume that because you the leader have got the vision burned into your heart that everyone else in the church has it too. People think about their own personal needs most of the time and you have to bring your church's common cause (vision) to the forefront on a regular basis. To you it may sound repetitious, but not to the average congregant.

You might want to use the offering envelope to communicate both Scripture and the church's vision and mission. The weekly bulletin could do the same. A monthly PowerPoint, video, or photo presentation at offering time for a minute could also expose various aspects of the ministry's vision to the congregation. Not too much, nor too little. Avoid overloading the congregation with too much detail so that they cannot see the big picture of what you are presenting. A well-prepared presentation by an associate and or a respected and trusted elder or board member also works well. Use your website as well as a tool to expose your vision and mission. A clear and simple presentation is better than something that is long and drawn out.

Exhort with Testimonies

Exhort the congregation with qualified testimonies of God's faithfulness in the area of finances. Testimonies encourage faith for the hearer to trust God for themselves in similar situations. Celebrate small and big victories alike, otherwise the 'super' testimonies can become discouraging for some.

Choose people from all walks of life, single moms, laborers, and business people etc, to show that not only ministers can enjoy God's financial blessings. These testimonies could also be printed up in your bulletin, or recorded and even projected if they have been previously videotaped. Whatever you do to exhort your people in their giving, do it with a high level of integrity, with conviction and without shame. God gets the glory when His people testify of His goodness in these practical areas. People see how the Word is working in the lives of ordinary people like them and they are encouraged to trust God for themselves for financial breakthrough.

Reach people at the spiritual level they are at, do not assume that they have your background in the scriptures. Be an encourager by using the 'Money Moments' to inspire faith.

Establish Giving As an Act of Worship

Establish giving at offering time as an act of worship. The congregation must not see tithe and offering time as mere 'bucket or basket' plunking. Giving must become a holy worshipful moment not to be passed over in some embarrassing way. Encourage obedience in this area with confidence and boldness. Avoid passing over the moment without first sharing a short exhortation from Scripture followed with a faith–filled declaration of devotion to God.

The 'Money Moments' you find in Section C and D are outlines you could use in your own way in your services. Remember, the emphasis in your people's thinking must shift from one where they see the preacher asking for money to a holy moment where God is worshipped with their substance.

The following account of God's deliverance of His people from Egypt shows how the people of Israel were to lay their first fruits at the feet of the priest and offer them to the Lord as an act of worship with rejoicing.

> So the LORD brought us out of Egypt with a mighty hand and with an outstretched arm, with great terror and with signs and wonders. He has brought us to this place and has given us this land, a land flowing with milk and honey; and now, behold, I have brought the firstfruits of the land which you, O LORD, have given me. Then you shall set it before the LORD your God, and worship before the LORD your God. So you shall rejoice in every good thing which the LORD your God has given to you and your house.

> Deuteronomy 26:8–11

Giving is clearly seen to be an act of worship before the Lord, celebrated with joy for all the good God has done. As a leader, set the tone at offering time by making it positive and filled with a corporate faith that pleases and honors God.

Equip Your People with Resources

Equip your people to become financially healthy God's way. Use the material in Section E: Useful Resource Material on page 189. The three subsections: Biblical

Stewardship, Tithes and Offerings, and Additional Scriptures by Topic are valuable outlines for strengthening your people in the area of stewardship. The Bible literally has more to say about practical financial matters than some of the doctrines that preachers preach week in and week out. It speaks of debt recovery, priorities, and responsibilities to the poor, stewardship, sacrificial giving, and so much more. You might find it useful once you have broken some barriers to conduct an annual 'Financial Focus' series. Many ministries make a variety of other resources available to their people through books, tapes, CDs and DVD, online links, workbook outlines on budgeting, etc. When your people see your commitment to their financial well–being is genuine and unashamed; they will receive these resources gladly.

Topics you might want to make available could include:

- How to get out of credit card debt
- How to establish a personal or family budget
- The difference between tithes and offerings
- What our responsibility is to the poor and needy
- How to invest for the future
- The list can go on to cover a variety of practical insights to daily living the Word of God deals with.

SECTION B

Money Moment Practicalities

Who Should Receive the Tithes and Offerings?

Certainly persons in leadership should receive tithes and offerings on behalf of the church. Usually the pastor or ministry leader is the most visible and respected authority figure. Sometimes it may be suitable to share the load with others anointed to lead and equip alongside the primary leader. It is important for the congregation to have confidence in its leadership, and when they work together as a team, confidence rises. You might want to consider a rotation or monthly pattern where the senior pastor takes the lead in this, but delegates this responsibility to others so the load can be shared, as well as to provide variety and new insights.

When Should Tithes and Offerings Be Received?

Some churches receive tithes and offerings at all their public meetings so that those congregants who only attend certain meetings can have their opportunity to participate in giving to the ministry. They don't want to leave anyone out. In cases where many attend multiple meetings, make them feel relaxed, by noting that 'some may have already given this week and we include you in today's 'prayer and faith declaration'.

As to what point in the meeting to actually pass the buckets or receptacles, some may want this part of the service to connect with the worship or song service. At this time, an atmosphere of worship is already set, and if the transition between singing and worshiping God with our substance is handled sensitively, things will 'flow' in the Spirit.

However some pastors prefer to be sure that all attendees are actually seated in the service. Some people arrive late and need to hear and receive the Word before being given an opportunity to give tithes and offerings. So tithes and offerings are received towards the end of the service. There is no absolute pattern here. The bottom line is that all the people must be equipped with the Word on giving; be challenged to honor God with their substance, and given an opportunity to do so.

How Should Tithes and Offerings Be Received?

Practically, this should be done in the most efficient and practical way. The people should be seated and focused on the matter at hand. If you have the people standing, it is difficult to write out checks or fill out offering envelopes. Giving levels are actually lower when these practical considerations are not taken into account.

Most churches use ushers, buckets, baskets, or bags. You might want to use the opportunity to make announcements or show special projections as the receptacles are being passed around. Others prefer to play music or have a special song item delivered at this time. Once again, be sure that this moment is an unashamed declaration of God's goodness and will in this matter of financial support. Offering time when conducted with an attitude of honor and reverence is worshipful. To worship means to 'ascribe worth to something or someone'. Avoid being 'religious' and contrived at times like these. Settle your heart and be bold when it comes to finances.

In ancient temple times, giving and the offering of sacrifices were out in public for all to see. On one occasion, Jesus even called his disciples over to examine what was going on and pointedly showed them who was giving and even how much! (Mark 11:41–44)

Some pastors feel that if they don't know who is giving what, they will remain pure and uninfluenced by who is giving. I have yet to meet a pastor who does not know who the big givers in the church are. Purity is not a matter of ignorance, pretended or otherwise, but of a heart that has been purged of improper motives. Let the Lord cleanse you of any intimidation or impurity yourself. Think about it, Paul counsels young Timothy to command those who are rich in the church to play their part. He would obviously have to know first that they are rich, and then second how much they are giving (1 Timothy 6:17–19).

Faithful stewards ought to know what is going on with the resources at hand as they are called to give an account for the resources at their disposal. (Of course many ministries have a team that works together on this to provide godly accountability and security: the pastor, cashier, bookkeeper, accountant, financial officer, board, etc.).

Envelopes, Bulletins, Credit Cards, and More

Many churches use an offering envelope to communicate Scriptures on the subject of giving. Others include portions of their mission statement on four variations of the same envelope. This highlights the mission of the church on a regular basis. They also include a

'Money Moment' segment in the weekly bulletin to further educate and communicate God's will concerning financial stewardship. The envelopes also include details of credit card giving. This may be controversial to you, but many people in today's modern generation see credit cards as a convenient way to handle their money in almost all of their transactions. They generally don't carry around much cash and sometimes even avoid writing checks. Certainly don't encourage them to get into debt in giving to God. A card is simply a convenient cash alternative to manage money.

Online internet giving is another innovation. During the church service you can include online givers in your prayer at offering time. When technology is harnessed for the spreading of the gospel it is a good thing. In the end it is all about the heart. If your heart is right, the means by which money changes hands is not the issue!

The Money Moment during the Worship Service

You might find it useful at offering time to have what we call a 'Money Moment', where the congregation is presented with the aid of a short PowerPoint (slideshow) exhortation on financial stewardship and giving. The 'Money Moment' consists of a Scripture reference, followed by two or at most three points related directly to that Scripture, and then an opportunity for the congregation to worship God with a declaration of their faith and devotion. This can be done in approximately three to four minutes and highlights the value God places on this subject. When you or someone you delegate to do the 'Money Moment' takes too long over this part of the service, you run the risk of overloading the congregation with too much information. Be wise in this. Manage and oversee this important aspect so that it flows with the rest of the worship service.

The 'Money Moment' should be front and center at this time in order to properly honor God. If you consider and administer this moment with reservation and hesitation, the congregation is likely to adopt a similar attitude in their giving.

This book presents you with many examples of 'Money Moments' to use or adapt to your particular style and circumstances.

After Tithes and Offerings Are Received

It is advisable to properly steward the resources released to your ministry with practices that satisfy God's Word and the law of the land. Be sure to have proper accountability measures in place with counting, recording, and disbursing funds. Make practical arrangements to carry off and safely store funds received during a service. Security may not seem be a big issue to start with, but as your church grows it will become very important. Select at least three trusted people other than family members to count and sign off against what has been received before forwarding to a trained bookkeeper, cashier or accountant responsible for church finances for processing and banking. (As the church grows in size you may need to enlarge this group for logistic purposes).

All these measures will play their part in instilling confidence in your members, partners, and supporters.

Some churches show the weekly or monthly giving in their bulletins as an accountability measure. This might not be suitable in your case, but at least on a monthly basis get the congregation to agree in a moment of unified consecration to invoke God's blessing on the giving of the whole church.

> Speak thus to the Levites, and say to them: 'When you take from the children of Israel the tithes which I have given you from them as your inheritance, then you shall offer up a heave offering of it to the LORD, a tenth of the tithe.
>
> Numbers 18:26–27

As the modern–day Levites or ministers, we are exhorted to give to worthy ministries and missions at least a tenth of all income received each month. In the church I pastored, we even held up the checks and prayed over them before they were sent out at the end of the month. The congregation knew who we supported and by how much. The rest we used on administering our own ministry. We did not consider local outreach efforts as part of our tithe, only what we gave away to other ministries. We considered it as unto the Lord and not for own benefit. You might want to use your website to highlight the ministries you give to with photos, descriptions etc.

A Word on the Spirit and Letter of Giving

Encouraging a lifestyle of giving is a matter of the heart. When your heart is right, your hand willingly does what God requires. When we are willing and obedient, God is pleased to bless us with the 'fat of the land' (Genesis 45:18). When people who do not have a good heart attitude are cajoled into giving, a bad taste is left in everyone's mouth. Faith is of the heart, and it comes as the Word is shared with integrity and conviction. We enter into the joy of giving when life is ministered through the Spirit and not through some legalistic formula. Privately in prayer ask the Lord to enlighten the congregation as to the hope of their calling in this area (Ephesians 1:18).

When we understand God's will and ways, we can easily partake of His nature through His precious promises (2 Peter 1:1–4). Giving then becomes a part of who we are, not merely what we sometimes do! In short, we give because of who we have become, not because we are told to follow some rule or formula. Our giving becomes part of a worship lifestyle that touches God's heart and opens His hand.

Weightier matters and Financial Stewardship

Woe to you, scribes and Pharisees, hypocrites! For you pay tithe of mint and anise and cumin, and have neglected the weightier matters of the law: justice and mercy and faith. These you ought to have done, without leaving the others undone.

Matthew 23:23

In this passage, Jesus shows us that we ought to have balance in our ministry. Some folks go overboard on the material side of things while others almost totally neglect stewardship teaching. Trust the Lord to be led by his Word and Spirit to provide a harmonious balance between the weightier matters and the vital areas of financial stewardship.

The Money Moment Explained

Each 'Money Moment' ought to have one Scripture as a foundation, two or three points of clarification or exhortation, and a declaration of faith and devotion connected to the scripture. The tithes and offerings are to be publicly presented to the Lord as He is our High Priest of the New Covenant, and we receive the congregation's gifts on His behalf. It is His money, not ours. We are the ones who collect, count, bank and spend it, but it is still His to direct, and He should be formally honored at this time.

An example of the 'Money Moment':
A Scripture with a title that summarizes a key point

God's Delight in Our Prosperity
Psalm 35:27

Let them shout for joy and be glad,
Who favor my righteous cause;
And let them say continually,
"Let the LORD be magnified,
Who has pleasure in the prosperity of his servant."

Points that could be made:

- Giving in support of God's righteous cause is reason for rejoicing.

- We are to continually declare or say out loud that God takes pleasure in or delights in our prosperity.

You could add to, adapt, or even amplify your own points from the verse. Then when the congregation has reflected on what has been said and been given an opportunity to prepare their tithes and offerings (writing checks, filling out envelopes, etc), lead them in a bold, out–loud declaration of faith and devotion as they give to the Lord and His work:

Dear Lord,
We rejoice in this opportunity to favor Your righteous cause with our tithes and offerings. We magnify You as you take pleasure in our prosperity. In Jesus name, amen.

Then go ahead and have the ushers/deacons receive the offering whilst the worship team leads in a song or instrumental. The congregation should be encouraged to remain seated as it is easier to write checks and fill out offering envelopes whilst seated.

Adapting the Money Moment

Each minister has his or her own style, so it is important to be free to adapt the 'Money Moment' so that it becomes part of the natural delivery. Communicating

God's will on finances is not only a matter of technique, but a natural expression of what you have adopted into the heart of your ministry. Ministering the Word on giving must always be from the heart.

You may want to set the context of each passage without being too involved. The 'Money Moment' is just that, a moment to hear and reflect on what the Word says about our finances. It probably should not become a long teaching which could overwhelm some, especially those that are young in the Lord and still growing.

Special Days in the Calendar

You might find it useful to use suitable 'Money Moments' that connect with annual days of celebration like Mother's Day and Father's Day. Other national days of remembrance are included in Section D.

Please note that each month has only four 'Money Moments'. With the special days in yearly cycle, there will be enough resources to cover the five weekend months in the year. The annual cycle could easily be repeated as your people would have had a whole year between repeats.

Using the Money Moment

Use the 'Money Moments' as your own weekly devotional focus on money matters, or whenever the tithes and offerings are received each week. It can even be adapted as a weekly blog posting to correspond with the 'Money Moment' that was delivered at the weekend church service. Make the book available to your leaders in your youth, young adults, ladies, men's ministry etc., so they can all be on the 'same page'. You might want to get a copy for your board members, and associate pastors if you have them.

SECTION C

Money Moments

January
God Is the Source of Our Blessing

The Bible clearly shows that God is the source of all our provision and blessing. He made the earth and all that is in it. Without His mercy and grace in our lives, we would not be able to do anything. He should be acknowledged, thanked, and worshiped for being our source. Also, our natural abilities, talents, and gifts that help us generate income all come from Him in the first place. We should not see our jobs as our **source** of supply, but rather as **channels** that God uses to bless us. He is our Father and gives us our daily bread!

Week 1

God is the Source of All Our Supply
1 Chronicles 29:14

But who am I, and who are my people,
That we should be able to offer so willingly as this?
For all things come from You,
And of Your own we have given You.

- God is the source of all our blessings.
- What we give back to him was his to start with.

"Dear Lord,
We honor you as the source of all our supply.
We recognize it all belongs to you.
We worship you with that which you honored us
with. Amen."

Notes:

Week 2

He Owns It All
Psalm 24:1

The earth is the Lord's, and all its fullness,
The world and those who dwell therein.

- The earth's fullness and abundance belongs to God.
- We are privileged to utilize all its fullness for his glory.

"Dear Lord,
Thank you for blessing us with the earth's fullness.
We commit to glorify you with what we us. Amen."

Notes:

Week 3

We Are Accountable As Stewards
Psalm 115:16

The heaven, even the heavens, are the Lord's;
But the earth he has given to the children of men.

- As the creator, God owns the heavens and the earth. We are given the earth to manage or steward to His glory.

- We are thus accountable to God for what we do with our resources.

- His Word teaches us our responsibilities: tithing, offerings, giving to the poor.

"Dear Lord,
Thank you for giving us the earth and its resources.
We desire to manage them in line with your Word.
Receive our tithes and offerings as our worship.
Amen."

Notes:

Week 4

God Wants Us to Enjoy All That He Gives
1 Timothy 6:17

Command those who are rich in this present age not to be haughty, nor to trust in uncertain riches but in the living God, who gives us richly all things to enjoy.

- We must trust in the Lord and not our riches.
- What we have comes from God in the first place.
- Proper trust leads to true enjoyment.

"Dear Lord,
We commit to properly trust in you and not riches.
Help us to truly enjoy what you have given us.
Amen."

Notes:

_____

_____

_____

_____

_____

_____

_____

_____

_____

_____

_____

_____

_____

_____

_____

_____

_____

_____

February
Giving As an Act of Worship

Offering time is as sacred as any other time in a service or a person's life. If you devalue offering time by quickly passing over it, you rob God of the worship He deserves. When you understand the value or worth God puts on practical financial matters, you will do the same. You will attach worth to your giving. Giving will become an integral part of your worship, just as prayer and singing is part of worship. Worship is always expressed in word and deed, so it is proper at offering time to worship God with our tithes and offerings.

Week 1

Worship the Lord with Your First Fruits
Deuteronomy 26:8–11

So the Lord *brought us out of Egypt…*
He has brought us to this place and has given us
this land, a land flowing with milk and honey; and
now, behold, I have brought the firstfruits of the land
which you, O Lord, have given me.
Then you shall set it before the Lord your God, and
worship before the Lord your God.

- Recognize God as the one who brings you out of bondage and gives us every good thing in the land.

- Bring your first fruits and set them before the Lord as your worship.

"Dear Lord,
You brought us into a land of abundance.
We rejoice in your goodness and we set our first fruits
before you today as our worship. Amen."

Notes:

_____

_____

_____

_____

_____

_____

_____

_____

_____

_____

_____

_____

_____

_____

_____

_____

_____

_____

_____

_____

_____

Week 2

Celebrate God's Presence with Joyful Giving
2 Samuel 6:13–15

And so it was, when those bearing the ark of the Lord *had gone six paces, that he sacrificed oxen and fatted sheep. Then David danced before the Lord with all his might; and David was wearing a linen ephod. So David and all the house of Israel brought up the ark of the* Lord *with shouting and with the sound of the trumpet.*

- King David sacrificed plenteously as an offering.
- He mixed his giving with dancing, shouting, and music to celebrate the return of God's presence.

"Dear Lord,
We celebrate your presence with our offering today.
We rejoice in your goodness with exuberant praise:
Dancing, shouting, and music. Amen."

Notes:

Week 3

Giving glorifies God
Psalm 96:8–9

Give to the Lord the glory due his name;
Bring an offering, and come into his courts.
Oh, worship the Lord in the beauty of holiness!

- It is proper to approach God with an offering.

- When we do, our giving becomes a holy act of worship and not merely a practical budget necessity!

"Dear Lord,
We worship you with our tithes and offerings.
May our giving be beautiful and holy to You. Amen."

Notes:

_____

_____

_____

_____

_____

_____

_____

_____

_____

_____

_____

_____

_____

_____

_____

_____

_____

_____

Week 4

Increase through Praise
Psalm 67:5–6

Let the peoples praise You, O God;
Let all the peoples praise You.
Then the earth shall yield her increase;
God, our own God, shall bless us.

- God promises increase when we mix praise with our giving. Praise and increase are connected!

- When you trust God, you will be cheerful and praise him as you give.

"Dear Lord,
Thank you for promising increase as we praise you.
We praise you today with our tithes and offerings.
Amen."

Notes:

March
Generosity in Giving

God is generous, and we are called to become like Him. Our giving must therefore be marked by generosity. Man's natural tendency is to give as little as possible and keep as much as possible. Generosity has to be cultivated through obedience and faith. We are totally indebted to God for everything. Even the air we breathe was created by Him.

So to give in abundance is not a foreign thing. Nowhere is God described as mean, stingy, or cheap. Rather, He is rich, abundant in mercy, and endures no shortage. He is worthy of extravagant worship. There is no gift too large for God. Make it your life quest to give as much as you possibly can. In Jesus words, "It is more blessed to give than to receive" (Acts 20:35).

Week 1

No limits!
2 Chronicles 5:6

And King Solomon, and all the congregation of Israel who were assembled with him before the ark, were sacrificing sheep and oxen that could not be counted or numbered for multitude.

- God will receive our extravagant love, even if it seems to be excessive to some.
- There is nothing too good for God—no limits!

"Dear Lord,
As we pour out our love on you in this practical way, accept our tithes and offerings as our sacrifice of praise for the no limit love you have for us. Amen."

Notes:

Week 2

Cornelius, a Generous Giver
Acts 10:1–2

There was a certain man in Caesarea called Cornelius, a centurion of what was called the Italian Regiment, a devout man and one who feared God with all his household, who gave alms generously to the people, and prayed to God always.

- Cornelius was not only tough and devout but also generous!

- His devotion and generosity came up before God, and he was later rewarded when Peter personally preached to him and his household.

"Dear Lord,
May our generous giving to those in need come up before you as a memorial of your goodness.
We worship you with our giving. Amen."

Notes:

Week 3

From Just Enough to More than Enough
Exodus 36:5

The people bring much more than enough
for the service of the work which the Lord
commanded us to do.

- God had commanded them to build a tabernacle.
- They were inspired to bring more than enough.
- When we properly value God's work, we are open to give more than enough to his work.

"Dear Lord,
Our desire is to move beyond just–enough giving to
more–than–enough giving.
Help us to properly value what you are doing and
want to do in our midst. Amen."

Notes:

_____

_____

_____

_____

_____

_____

_____

_____

_____

_____

_____

_____

_____

_____

_____

_____

_____

_____

_____

_____

Week 4

The Fragrance of Your gift
John 12:3

*Then Mary took a pound of very costly oil of spike-
nard, anointed the feet of Jesus, and wiped his feet
with her hair. And the house was filled with the fragrance of the oil.*

- Jesus accepted Mary's costly gift.
- Our giving puts out a beautiful fragrance.
- Be sure your heart is right when you give.

"Dear Lord,
*May our giving fill your house with the fragrance of
generosity. Thank you for not holding back your best
when you sent Jesus. We love and adore you. Amen"*

Notes:

April
Money with a Mission

Everything God does has purpose built into it. Our prosperity ought to be attached to our purpose or calling in life. When we know why money comes to us, we will mange it properly. It will work for God's purposes. God has chosen His people to be channels of blessing to a world that does not know him. As our Father, He wants to show His goodness to a poverty–stricken world through us His children. We are ambassadors of goodness and grace.

Week 1

Blessed to Be a Blessing
Genesis 12:2

I will make you a great nation;
I will bless you and make your name great;
And you shall be a blessing.

- We must realize that in order to be a blessing to others, we have to first be blessed by God ourselves. Or to put it another way...

- God wants us to be channels of blessing in a divine flow of blessing.

"Dear Lord,
Help us not to be so narrow-minded about your plan.
You want us receive blessings and pass them on to
others us as we give. Amen."

Notes:

Week 2

Wealth to Establish His Covenant
Deuteronomy 8:18

You shall remember the Lord *your God, for it is he who gives you power to get wealth, that he may establish his covenant which he swore to your fathers, as it is this day.*

- Hard work is not enough in life. We need God's anointing to prosper.

- We also must realize that our wealth is given to us for a purpose: to establish God's covenant.

"Dear Lord,
We remember that it is you who anoints us to prosper. We willingly give our tithes and offerings today to establish your covenant. Amen."

Notes:

Week 3

Food in God's House
Malachi 3:10

Bring all the tithes into the storehouse,
That there may be food in My house,
And try Me now in this,"
Says the Lord of hosts,
"If I will not open for you the windows of heaven
And pour out for you such blessing
That there will not be room enough to receive it."

- Tithing makes sure that is ample supply in God's house: his church!

- Those that minister in his house have their needs supplied and are able to focus their ministry on meeting the needs of the saints.

- God rewards those that tithe to his house with overflowing blessing; windows of heaven are opened to them.

"Dear Lord,
I bring my tithes to your storehouse to provide for those who labor in it.
Thank you for rewarding me with open heavens and an overflowing blessing. Amen."

Notes:

_____

_____

_____

_____

_____

_____

_____

_____

_____

_____

_____

_____

_____

_____

_____

_____

_____

_____

Week 4

Abundance for Every Good Work
2 Corinthians 9:8

And God is able to make all grace abound toward you, that you, always having all sufficiency in all things, may have an abundance for every good work.

- God is able to make his grace or divine ability abound toward us.

- He wants us to have a sufficiency for ourselves, and ...

- An abundance for every good work too!

"Dear Lord,
We rejoice that you are a God of abundant supply.
We receive your abundance in our lives and minis-
tries. Our heart is to bless others with our abundance.
Amen."

Notes:

May
Priorities

In order to achieve His purposes in and through us, God establishes priorities. He is first interested in our hearts, so our personal relationship with Him must be our priority too. Any healthy relationship values what the other party values. God's hand will supply our needs, but it is only His heart that truly sustains life. Priorities establish order. When we do what is required first, the rest falls into place. We thus avoid playing unending catch up.

Week 1

Seek the Lord
2 Chronicles 26:5

He sought God in the days of Zechariah, who had understanding in the visions of God; and as long as he sought the Lord, God made him prosper.

- King Uzziah sought the Lord.
- As long as he did, God made him to prosper.
- God will reward our hunger for him.

"Dear Lord,
We seek your face as our first ministry.
Thank you for the promised prosperity as our reward.
Amen."

Notes:

_____

_____

_____

_____

_____

_____

_____

_____

_____

_____

_____

_____

_____

_____

_____

_____

_____

_____

_____

_____

Week 2

Seek God's kingdom first
Matthew 6:32–34

For after all these things the Gentiles seek. For your heavenly Father knows that you need all these things. But seek first the kingdom of God and his righteousness, and all these things shall be added to you.

- God knows what we need.
- He wants us to properly prioritize our lives and focus on his kingdom purposes first.
- Our needs will follow in order and be added.

"Dear Lord,
We know you care about us.
We choose to put your kingdom purposes first.
As we focus our priorities, thank you for promising to add to our lives all that we need. Amen."

Notes:

_____

_____

_____

_____

_____

_____

_____

_____

_____

_____

_____

_____

_____

_____

_____

_____

_____

_____

_____

_____

Week 3

First Fruits or Leftovers?
Proverbs 3:9–10

*Honor the Lord with your possessions, and with the
first fruits of all your increase;
So your barns will be filled with plenty,
And your vats will overflow with new wine.*

- Our giving honors the Lord and is an act of worship.

- When we give our first fruits and not our leftovers, we sanctify (protect) the remaining ninety percent.

- After obeying, we can release our faith and expect God to bless us as he promises.

*"Dear Lord,
With honor and worship we present the first fruits of
all our increase.
You have promised to bless our obedience with over-
flowing plenty.
We consecrate our first fruits to you, expecting your
blessing on our finances this month.
In Jesus name, amen."*

Notes:

Week 4

Solomon asks for wisdom
1 Kings 3:12–13

Behold, I have done according to your words; see, I have given you a wise and understanding heart, so that there has not been anyone like you before you, nor shall any like you arise after you. And I have also given you what you have not asked: both riches and honor, so that there shall not be anyone like you among the kings all your days.

- Solomon asked for wisdom to fulfill his commission as king.

- He got it and in addition was rewarded with what he had not asked God for: riches and honor.

- When our hearts are right, God blesses over and above.

*"Dear Lord,
We set our hearts right before you today. Give us the wisdom we need to fulfill our callings in Christ. Amen."*

Notes:

_____

_____

_____

_____

_____

_____

_____

_____

_____

_____

_____

_____

_____

_____

_____

_____

_____

_____

_____

June
Sowing and Reaping

Sowing and reaping is a kingdom principle that works whether you like it or not. God sowed his Son into the world expecting to receive back an abundant harvest of souls. In turn, we sow our seed with the same expectancy. Our time, talent, and financial resources are what are in our hands. We must choose to attach a mission to our money: to further the gospel around the world. God wants us to believe Him for increase like any farmer who sows seed for the purpose of producing a harvest of increase.

Week 1

The Law of Sowing and Reaping
Genesis 8:22

While the earth remains,
Seedtime and harvest,
Cold and heat,
Winter and summer,
And day and night
Shall not cease.

- We cannot ignore the law of sowing and reaping.

- In order to reap a harvest, we have to sow.

- Praying for a harvest is useless unless you have sown.

"Dear Lord,
Thank you for showing us the importance of sowing.
As we sow today, we know that a harvest will follow
our obedience. Amen."

Notes:

_____

_____

_____

_____

_____

_____

_____

_____

_____

_____

_____

_____

_____

_____

_____

_____

_____

_____

_____

Week 2

Seed to the Sower
2 Corinthians 9:10

Now may he who supplies seed to the sower, and bread for food, supply and multiply the seed you have sown and increase the fruits of your righteousness.

- God will give both seed for you to sow and bread for your food.

- We have the task of separating what is seed and what is to be used for our bread or needs.

- God will multiply the seed we sow but not the food we eat.

"Dear Lord,
We purpose to be sowers of seed, not merely consumers of bread.
Lead us by your Spirit in our sowing.
Thank you for this way of multiplying the fruits of our righteousness. Amen."

Notes:

Week 3

Sowing for Increase
Luke 6:38

Give, and it will be given to you: good measure, pressed down, shaken together, and running over will be put into your bosom. For with the same measure that you use, it will be measured back to you.

- God promises an abundant return on our giving.
- The measure of our giving determines our return.

"Dear Lord,
Thank you for your generosity toward us.
May we become more and more like you as we give generously to your work. Amen."

Notes:

Week 4

Reaping in Due Season
Galatians 6:9

And let us not grow weary while doing good, for in due season we shall reap if we do not lose heart.

- There is always a season to sow and to harvest.
- Patience or continued obedience is needed to ensure a harvest.

"Dear Lord,
As we continue to do good, we are assured that we will reap in due season.
Strengthen us to stand in faith without fainting.
Amen."

Notes:

July
Heart Matters

When your heart is right before God, you will have no problem sowing for and managing increase. Greed and covetousness are not part of the new creation. When you are full of God, you will hold onto what you have with a light grip. It is only the unrenewed mind steeped in fear and negative religious tradition that cannot handle wealth. Worship God and allow Him to change your heart. Ask Him for a largeness of heart like the sands of the seashore. Been to the beach lately and seen how much sand there is?

Week 1

Willing and Obedient
Isaiah 1:19

If you are willing and obedient,
You shall eat the good of the land.

- Obedience is good and speaks of the hand.
- Willingness is better and speaks of the heart.

"Dear Lord,
We obey from our hearts as we serve in your kingdom.
Amen."

Notes:

Week 2

The Love of Money versus the Love of God
1 Timothy 6:10

For the love of money is a root of all kinds of evil, for which some have strayed from the faith in their greediness, and pierced themselves through with many sorrows.

- The love of money is evil, not money itself.
- Misplaced love (of money), greed, and sorrow are all connected.

"Dear Lord,
We love and put our trust in you, not our money.
We want to have a loose hold on our money so that we can be ready to give. Amen."

Notes:

_____

_____

_____

_____

_____

_____

_____

_____

_____

_____

_____

_____

_____

_____

_____

_____

_____

Week 3

Giving from a Generous Heart
2 Corinthians 9:5

Prepare your generous gift beforehand, which you had previously promised, that it may be ready as a matter of generosity and not as a grudging obligation.

- God is pleased when we give from a heart of generosity.

- When we prepare beforehand to give, we do not feel under the pressure of the moment and thus avoid giving as a grudging obligation.

"Dear Lord,
Help us to plan our giving so that we can give from a generous heart. Amen."

Notes:

Week 4

Largeness of Heart
1 Kings 4:29

And God gave Solomon wisdom and exceedingly great understanding, and largeness of heart like the sand on the seashore.

- Small–hearted people are usually stingy, operating mostly out of fear of lack or doing without.

- Large–hearted people are usually generous and operate mostly in faith that God's supply will never run dry!

*"Dear Lord,
Give us largeness of heart that we might be generous in our giving. Amen."*

Notes:

August
Principles of Work

God will not do what we are expected to do, and we cannot do what only He can do. Blessing involves a divine interchange. Our faith without works is dead. He blesses the work of our hands, not the seat of our pants. Many try in vain to invoke God's blessing without being diligent. Others work hard but do not invoke His favor by means of their faith. Both fall short of God's best. Learn to cooperate with God in your work.

Week 1

Heartily to the Lord
Colossians 3:23

Whatever you do, do your work heartily,
as for the Lord, rather than for men.

- God wants us to properly value our work.

- Our heart attitude ought to be pleasing to him.

"Dear Lord,
We choose to properly value our work.
May we work as to you from the heart.
I cheerfully honor give the fruit of my labor towards
the extension of your kingdom. Amen."

Notes:

_____

_____

_____

_____

_____

_____

_____

_____

_____

_____

_____

_____

_____

_____

_____

_____

_____

_____

_____

_____

_____

_____

Week 2

Planning, Diligence, and Plenty
Proverbs 21:5

The plans of the diligent lead surely to plenty,
But those of everyone who is hasty, surely to poverty.

- Planning and diligence produce plenty.
- Hasty financial decisions lead to poverty.
- Prosperity is not a matter of chance but of choice.

"Dear Lord,
Help us to be diligent in our giving, planning, and
conduct.
As we wait upon you for wisdom, guide us toward
plenty and keep us from poverty.
We commit not to be hasty in our financial decision
making. Amen."

Notes:

Week 3

Your Hands Tell a Story
Proverbs 10:4

He who has a slack hand becomes poor,
But the hand of the diligent makes rich.

- Slackness and diligence both have consequences.
- We have the power to choose between being slack or diligent.
- Our daily routine makes a difference.

"Dear Lord,
Help us understand that our actions will always have consequences sooner or later.
May our hands be diligent. Amen."

Notes:

_____

_____

_____

_____

_____

_____

_____

_____

_____

_____

_____

_____

_____

_____

_____

_____

_____

_____

_____

_____

Week 4

The Tiny Ant Tells a Big Story
Proverbs 6:6–8

Go to the ant, you sluggard!
Consider her ways and be wise,
Which, having no captain,
Overseer or ruler,
Provides her supplies in the summer,
And gathers her food in the harvest.

- Ants work without being driven by outside motivation.
- Ants do what is needed now to provide for their future needs.

"Dear Lord,
May we humbly learn diligence and industry from the ant. Strengthen us to do today what is needed to provide for tomorrow. Amen."

Notes:

September
The Lifestyle of Giving

The law of gravity does not work only when the conditions are right. Our giving must not be attached to how good things are, or how we feel at any one time. When we become committed to God's ways, we will give in all seasons, not just when things are going well. We are to walk by faith, not by what we see in the economy. Make giving a lifelong habit, no matter the circumstances.

Week 1

Cast Your Bread on Every Wave
Ecclesiastes 11:1, 4, 6

Cast your bread upon the waters,
For you will find it after many days ...
He who observes the wind will not sow,
And he who regards the clouds will not reap ...
In the morning sow your seed,
And in the evening do not withhold your hand;
For you do not know which will prosper,
Either this or that,
Or whether both alike will be good.

- Give from conviction, not convenience.

- Do not look at natural conditions—the wind and clouds—they will not always be favorable.

- Keep sowing because you are committed to a lifestyle of giving, no matter what!

"Dear Lord,
We chose to be faithful in our giving no matter the circumstances.
We give because we are convinced it is right to do so and trust you to reward our diligence. Amen."

Notes:

_____

_____

_____

_____

_____

_____

_____

_____

_____

_____

_____

_____

_____

_____

_____

_____

_____

_____

_____

Week 2

Giving Is Right Even When Things Are Tight
Mark 12:42–44

Then one poor widow came and threw in two mites ... So he called his disciples to himself and said to them, "Assuredly, I say to you that this poor widow has put in more than all those who have given to the treasury; for they all put in out of their abundance, but she out of her poverty put in all that she had, her whole livelihood."

- The Lord watches what we do with our giving.

- The Lord wants you to give even if you are poor because it opens the door to you being blessed.

- The Lord will reward even your small gift, because to you it is proportionately big.

"Dear Lord,
We give because it is right to give. Whether from abundance or lack, we rejoice in your goodness to us. We are confident that you will meet our every need according to your riches in glory. Amen."

Notes:

Week 3

Isaac Sowed in Famine and Reaped
Genesis 26:1, 12

*There was a famine in the land, besides the first fam-
ine that was in the days of Abraham. And Isaac went
to Abimelech king of the Philistines, in Gerar...
Then Isaac sowed in that land, and reaped in the
same year a hundredfold; and the Lord blessed him.*

- There was a famine in the land where a person would be tempted to hold onto what he had.

- Yet Isaac obeyed God, stayed put, sowed his seed, and reaped an abundance in the same year!

- He did it in faith, and God rewarded his commitment in the face of adverse circumstances.

*"Dear Lord,
Help us to obey when it seems all wrong to sow our
seed. Renew our minds to your supernatural ability to
grant us increase even in famine times. Amen."*

Notes:

Week 4

Scatter in Order to Increase
Proverbs 11:24

There is one who scatters, yet increases more;
And there is one who withholds more than is right,
But it leads to poverty.

- Continue to sow your financial seed even when it looks like it is just being scattered.

- God sees you commitment and consistency and will cause it to increase.

"Dear Lord,
We continue to sow our seed. Thank you for the faith to do so and for delivering us from a withholding spirit. Amen."

Notes:

_____

_____

_____

_____

_____

_____

_____

_____

_____

_____

_____

_____

_____

_____

_____

_____

_____

_____

_____

_____

October
Supporting God's Work

God is not a counterfeiter, dropping money over the balconies of heaven to support ministries that are committed to His mission to reach the world. No, He requires our participation. The Holy Spirit works together with us as we obey. If He worked in a vacuum, our giving would be unnecessary. God's Word shows a variety of purposes that our giving serves.

Week 1

Heaven's Windows
Malachi 3:10

Bring all the tithes into the storehouse,
That there may be food in My house,
And try Me now in this,"
Says the LORD *of hosts,*
"If I will not open for you the windows of heaven
And pour out for you such blessing
That there will not be room enough to receive it.

- We should bring our tithes into the local storehouse or church so that the needs of the ministers in that house are met.

- God promises to reward our obedience in supporting his ministers.

- There will be abundance in our lives too.

"Dear Lord,
I count it a privilege to bring my tithes into your storehouse. I identify with and support your work in my local church.
Thank you for the promise of blessing in my life in return for my obedience. Amen."

Notes:

Week 2

From Their Substance
Luke 8:1–3

*He went through every city and village, preaching
and bringing the glad tidings of the kingdom of God.
And the twelve were with him, and certain women
who had been healed of evil spirits and infirmities—
Mary called Magdalene, out of whom had come seven
demons, and Joanna the wife of Chuza, Herod's
steward, and Susanna, and many others who provided for him from their substance.*

- Jesus' followers included women prepared to leave all and follow him.
- They came from the highest in society to the lowest.
- They provided for him from their substance.

*"Dear Lord,
Thank you for including me in your company.
I willingly support your work from my substance.
May my giving please you today. Amen."*

Notes:

Week 3

Building the House
1 Chronicles 29:3–4

Moreover, because I have set my affection on the house of my God, I have given to the house of my God, over and above all that I have prepared for the holy house, my own special treasure of gold and silver.

- King David gave toward the building of the temple from his own special treasure because he had "set his affection" on God's house.

- Giving to build God's house is all about affection.

"Dear Lord,
As we give today, we desire from our hearts to see your house built. We love and appreciate all that you are to us. Amen."

Notes:

_____

_____

_____

_____

_____

_____

_____

_____

_____

_____

_____

_____

_____

_____

_____

_____

_____

_____

_____

_____

_____

Week 4

Standing By Others in the Body of Christ
Acts 11:27–30

And in these days prophets came from Jerusalem to Antioch. Then one of them, named Agabus, stood up and showed by the Spirit that there was going to be a great famine throughout all the world, which also happened in the days of Claudius Caesar. Then the disciples, each according to his ability, determined to send relief to the brethren dwelling in Judea.

- The people in Antioch were moved to support God's people in Jerusalem even though they were to be affected by the same famine!

- Their selflessness is an inspiration for us today to be ready to support God's people where there is a need even in the face of our own need.

- For it is when we give from conviction, not convenience, that it will be given back to us.

"Dear Lord,
Thank you for showing us this selfless example of giving. We purpose to support your work wherever and whenever you lead us. Amen."

Notes:

November
Giving to the Needy

From God's point of view, no one really deserves what he or she gets. We have all fallen short of His glory because of sin, and His provision is therefore all about grace and mercy. Those that are blessed have what they have by God's grace. Those that do not have enough need His mercy. The blessed are called to be His instruments of mercy. Giving to the needy is an expression of God's goodness. This kind of giving promotes the softening of hard hearts. Mercy is intended to encourage repentance. Do not withhold mercy in this practical area, sow your seed with faith, and touch the hearts of the "untouchables".

Week 1

Consider the Poor
Psalm 41:1–3

Blessed is he who considers the poor;
The Lord will deliver him in time of trouble.
The Lord will preserve him and keep him alive,
And he will be blessed on the earth;
You will not deliver him to the will of his enemies.
The Lord will strengthen him on his bed of illness;
You will sustain him on his sickbed.

- The Lord promises to bless, deliver, preserve, and strengthen us in our need when we are prepared to consider or help the poor in their need.

"Dear Lord,
Thank you for coming to us in our poverty and need.
As we give of our substance to you today, open our
eyes that we may consider or help the poor the way
you do. Amen."

Notes:

_____

_____

_____

_____

_____

_____

_____

_____

_____

_____

_____

_____

_____

_____

_____

_____

_____

_____

_____

_____

_____

Week 2

Pity on the Poor
Proverbs 19:17

He who has pity on the poor lends to the Lord.
And he will pay back what he has given.

- We partner with God when we pity the poor.
- We learn his ways when we pity those less fortunate then us.
- As a bonus, he promises to make it up to us.

"Dear Lord,
We partner with you and take pity on the poor.
We humbly realize that we too need your pity.
Thank you for this opportunity to be a blessing to those less fortunate than us. Amen."

Notes:

Let us begin to systematically bless 1- Our widows.
2- Our orphens.
3- Those in the household of faith who are observing your principles but need help.
4- Those outside the household who need to see God's mercy demonstrated-

Week 3

Mercy on the Needy
Proverbs 14:31

He who oppresses the poor reproaches his Maker,
But he who honors him has mercy on the needy.

- We bring reproach on the Lord if we take advantage of the poor.

- We honor the Lord when we have mercy on the needy.

- Mercy is when you get something you don't necessarily deserve.

"Dear Lord,
You had mercy on us. We extend this mercy to those in need and honor you with our giving. Amen."

Notes:

_____

_____

_____

_____

_____

_____

_____

_____

_____

_____

_____

_____

_____

_____

_____

_____

_____

_____

_____

Week 4

Giving to the Poor
Proverbs 28:27

He who gives to the poor will not lack,
But he who hides his eyes will have many curses

- As we help the poor in their lack, God will help us in our area of lack.
- We bring a curse upon ourselves if we hide our eyes from helping the poor.

"Dear Lord,
You have said that I am not to hide my eyes from the difficulties of the poor.
Show me where I can be a blessing to them, and I thank you for the promise that as I obey you in this, I will not lack. Amen."

Notes:

_____

_____

_____

_____

_____

_____

_____

_____

_____

_____

_____

_____

_____

_____

_____

_____

_____

_____

_____

_____

December
God's Delight

God is delighted when we do well. As a loving Father, He is committed to our well–being. He is honored and glorified when His children are restored to peace and harmony within His will. Prosperity involves a harmony between spirit, soul, and body. Jesus went to the cross to open the way back into the Father's presence. In His presence is all the joy, strength and provision we could ever need.

Week 1

God's Delight
Psalm 35:27

Let them shout for joy and be glad,
Who favor my righteous cause;
And let them say continually,
"Let the Lord be magnified,
Who has pleasure in the prosperity of his servant."

- We can shout for joy and be glad because we favor God's righteous cause with our service and giving.

- God's delights in our well–being or prosperity.

"Dear Lord,
We thank you for the opportunity to favor your righteous cause with our giving.
We say continually that you take pleasure in our prosperity.
We magnify and bless your holy name. Amen."

Notes:

_____

_____

_____

_____

_____

_____

_____

_____

_____

_____

_____

_____

_____

_____

_____

_____

_____

_____

_____

_____

_____

Week 2

Prosper in all things
3 John 2

Beloved, I pray that you may prosper in all things and be in health, just as your soul prospers.

- John's prayer reveals God's heart for our prosperity.
- God wants us to do well in every area of life: spirit, soul, and body.

"Dear Lord,
Thank you for wanting us to do well in all areas of our lives, including our finances.
We bless you with our tithes and offerings. Amen."

Notes:

_____

_____

_____

_____

_____

_____

_____

_____

_____

_____

_____

_____

_____

_____

_____

_____

_____

_____

Week 3

Good Success
Joshua 1:8

This Book of the Law shall not depart from your mouth, but you shall meditate in it day and night, that you may observe to do according to all that is written in it. For then you will make your way prosperous, and then you will have good success.

- We have a responsibility to continually meditate or think about God's Word.
- He'll give us wisdom how to apply it in daily life.
- Success will follow our obedience to his Word.

"Dear Lord,
Thank you for your Word. You have promised good success as I meditate on it continually. Help me apply it daily so I can make my way prosperous. Amen."

Notes:

_____

_____

_____

_____

_____

_____

_____

_____

_____

_____

_____

_____

_____

_____

_____

_____

_____

_____

Week 4

For Our Sakes
2 Corinthians 8:9

For you know the grace of our Lord Jesus Christ, that he was rich, yet for your sakes he became poor, that you through his poverty might become rich.

- Jesus was our substitute on the cross.
- He became poor for our sakes so that we might be made rich (a full supply) to do God's will.

"Dear Lord,
Thank you for being our substitutionary sacrifice on the cross.
You gave us your riches and took our poverty.
We receive your full supply by faith and bless you for your goodness toward us. Amen."

Notes:

_____

_____

_____

_____

_____

_____

_____

_____

_____

_____

_____

_____

_____

_____

_____

_____

_____

SECTION D

Special and Annual Days

Easter

John 3:14–17

And as Moses lifted up the serpent in the wilderness, even so must the Son of Man be lifted up, that whoever believes in him should not perish but have eternal life. For God so loved the world that he gave his only begotten Son, that whoever believes in him should not perish but have everlasting life.

- In order for us to be able to give our lives to God, he had to give his life for us.

- God is the greatest giver the world has ever seen or ever will see. He gave his only begotten Son.

- This Easter, let's become more like him and be prepared to give our all to him.

"Dear Lord,
You gave your best for us.
Help us realize that we are to give our best for you.
Amen."

Notes:

Mother's Day

John 2:5–6

His mother said to the servants, "Whatever he says to you, do it." Now there were set there six waterpots of stone, according to the manner of purification of the Jews, containing twenty or thirty gallons apiece.

- Mary, Jesus' mother, had sense enough to instruct the servants in simple obedience.

- Jesus chose six pots of water totaling a maximum of 180 gallons! Quite a bit of wine for a wedding!

- God's provision is always abundantly more than enough.

"Dear Lord,
We give today from a heart of obedience.
Thank you for an abundant supply to meet our every need. Amen."

Notes:

Father's Day

Matthew 6:8–9

For your Father knows the things you have need of before you ask him.

- As our loving Father, God anticipates our need.
- Yet he still wants us to ask in faith and confidence in his revealed will for our provision.

"Dear Lord,
Thank you for making provision to supply our every need. We love you and ask today with confidence that you give us our daily bread. Amen."

Notes:

Christmas

Matthew 2:11–12

And when they (the wise men) had come into the house, they saw the young Child with Mary his mother, and fell down and worshiped him. And when they had opened their treasures, they presented gifts to him: gold, frankincense, and myrrh.

- The wise men made a huge effort to come before the Lord and present gifts appropriate for a King.
- Wise men still seek the Lord and worship him with their valuable gifts.

"Dear Lord,
We worship you this special day with our gifts.
Thank you for becoming the greatest gift we have ever received! Amen."

Notes:

_____

_____

_____

_____

_____

_____

_____

_____

_____

_____

_____

_____

_____

_____

_____

_____

_____

_____

_____

_____

_____

Culture Days

The following two examples are intended to encourage you to include your own special cultural days that are of significant Christian value to your own nation and community.

Independence Day (USA)

James 1:25

But he who looks into the perfect law of liberty and continues in it, and is not a forgetful hearer but a doer of the work, this one will be blessed in what he does.

- Liberty is not the absence of control. It is the establishment of love at the center of control.

- True liberty comes when we look into God's law and obey it. Blessing always follows obedience.

"Dear Lord,
Thank you for giving us your Word to set us free.
As we give today, we are blessed in what we do.
Amen."

Notes:

_____

_____

_____

_____

_____

_____

_____

_____

_____

_____

_____

_____

_____

_____

_____

_____

Thanksgiving (USA)

Psalm 107:8

Oh, that men would give thanks to the LORD *for his goodness,*
And for his wonderful works to the children of men!

- We have so much to be thankful for.
- Giving God thanks is a choice we make to honor him.

"Dear Lord,
We give thanks today for your goodness in our lives.
Every good thing comes from you, and we bless you today with our tithes and offerings. Amen."

Notes:

_____

_____

_____

_____

_____

_____

_____

_____

_____

_____

_____

_____

_____

_____

_____

_____

_____

_____

_____

Special Offerings

Special Speakers

Philippians 4:15, 19

*Now you Philippians know also that in the begin-
ning of the gospel, when I departed from Macedonia,
no church shared with me concerning giving and
receiving but you only…
And my God shall supply all your need according to
his riches in glory by Christ Jesus.*

- Support for traveling ministries and special speakers is special.
- It carries special blessing to both the visiting ministry and those ministered to.

*"Dear Lord,
As we support our special speaker today, we know
that we spread the blessings you give us.
Thank you for promising to meet our needs in return
for our sowing! Amen."*

Notes:

_____

_____

_____

_____

_____

_____

_____

_____

_____

_____

_____

_____

_____

_____

_____

_____

_____

_____

Building Fund Offering

Exodus 25:1–2, 8

Then the Lord *spoke to Moses, saying: "Speak to the children of Israel, that they bring Me an offering. From everyone who gives it willingly with his heart you shall take My offering...*
And let them make Me a sanctuary, that I may dwell among them."

- Any offering toward this building ought to be given willingly from the heart.

- This offering is given as to the Lord for his purposes.

"Dear Lord,
As we willingly give this offering toward this build-ing project, we do so to create a facility to house your corporate presence in our midst. May this offering be wisely used in this project. Amen."

Notes:

_____

_____

_____

_____

_____

_____

_____

_____

_____

_____

_____

_____

_____

_____

_____

_____

_____

_____

_____

Building Dedication

Numbers 7:1

When Moses had finished setting up the tabernacle, that he anointed it and consecrated it and all its furnishings, and the altar and all its utensils; so he anointed them and consecrated them.

- The tabernacle or place of meeting with God was anointed and consecrated, along with all its furnishings.

- Today, this facility is to be anointed and dedicated to the Lord's use by our faith.

"Dear Lord,
Thank you for providing this facility for our use.
We consecrate it for the use of the gospel and anoint everything in it for your glory. We rejoice in your mercy and bless you with all that is within us.
Amen."

Notes:

Impacting your Community and City

Acts 19:10

And this continued for two years, so that all who dwelt in Asia heard the word of the Lord Jesus, both Jews and Greeks.

- Paul's ministry impacted not only the whole city of Ephesus, but also the whole region of Asia Minor (modern–day Turkey).

- The local silversmith industry that made small idols was impacted by the outpouring of God's truth.

- It is God's will for the church in any city and region to impact all facets of society for good.

"Dear Lord,
As we consecrate these tithes and offerings, we trust you to give us favor in our city and region with all those in authority in government, law and order, education, medical services, business, media, sports, and entertainment.
Help us encourage godly entrepreneurship and pros-perity in our sphere of influence.
We know that when the righteous prospers, the city rejoices!
Amen."

Notes:

Continued Giving in Difficult Times

Genesis 26:12–14

Then Isaac sowed in that land, and reaped in the same year a hundredfold; and the LORD *blessed him. The man began to prosper, and continued prospering until he became very prosperous; for he had possessions of flocks and possessions of herds and a great number of servants. So the Philistines envied him.*

- Isaac sowed in a time of famine when most were content to withhold their seed.

- Because God's Word never changes, Isaac was rewarded for his faith as the Lord blessed him. He even became so rich that the Philistines envied him!

- God's best is for us to continue to be fruitful, even in difficult times.

"Dear Lord,
Thank you that we can trust you to prosper us even in difficult times. As we continue to be faithful in our sowing, we know that you will watch over us and cause our seed to grow, all to your glory.
Amen."

Notes:

_____

_____

_____

_____

_____

_____

_____

_____

_____

_____

_____

_____

_____

_____

_____

_____

_____

_____

SECTION E

Useful Resource Material

The resource material in this section can be used by anyone for their own edification and encouragement, or it could be used by the church or ministry leadership to equip their people in a financial focus teaching, or a preaching series or even a special seminar.

The first resource, entitled 'Biblical Stewardship: The Principles of Prosperity', is a concise and practical overview of God's financial plan for man. The second resource is an outline on the subject of 'Tithes and Offerings' that could be taught in series, posted up in a weekly series on the ministry's website or even printed on a special bulletin. Adapt and use it in any way you see fit.

For a free sample PowerPoint of a weekly 'Money Moment' that you could use to create your own template, go to www.moneymoment.org

Introduction

The Lord takes pleasure in the prosperity of his servant.

Psalm 35:27

Prosperity defined
Shalom: safety, welfare, peace

In a world ravaged by sin, sickness, and lack, God manifested his goodness toward us in the life and ministry of Jesus:

> I have come that they may have life, and that they may have it more abundantly.

John 10:10

If you are ever tempted to doubt, or at least wonder about the nature of God, look at Jesus. He perfectly represented the Father's nature and heart to us. God sent Jesus to share with us a quality of life that knows no lack or shortage. Do you ever see Jesus coming up short as He fulfilled His purpose? He always enjoyed a full supply of God's provision: spirit, soul, and body. As our example, we should be encouraged to walk in His ways and enjoy the same covenant provision in every area of our lives.

> Beloved, I pray that you may prosper in all things and be in health, just as your soul prospers.
>
> 3 John 1:2

The Apostle John, who knew the heart of God, prayed this Holy Spirit–inspired prayer. He had leaned his head on Jesus' breast at the Last Supper, having come to know and trust Him intimately as a close follower. John understood that there was no artificial separation between the well–being of the inner man from the outer man. He had seen Jesus meet people's internal spiritual needs, like forgiveness, as well as their external needs, like food. Only through man's tradition and religious unbelief do some people have a warped idea that God only cares about the inner soul of man. Prosperity or a state of well–being is not restricted merely to the soul, but includes provision for the outer man as well. Material well–being is part of being made whole through salvation.

The Bible definition of prosperity means to enjoy 'good success or a full supply'. It also means in the original languages of the Bible to be 'helped on your way'. I don't know of anyone who does not feel he or she could do with a little help on his or her way.

Another meaning is to 'push forward, break out, or to be profitable'. The peace, safety, and preservation that comes from receiving God's help in our daily affairs is something I know we could all enjoy more. God is our great helper, not the great hinderer. He gets glory when we do well in life. There is no glory for God in a broke, busted, and disgusted Christian stumbling forlorn along the sidewalks of life. Our Father does not mistreat anyone, let alone His children.

May this resource help you understand God's will concerning your prosperity and build up your faith so that you can begin trusting God in this vital area of your walk with the Lord. You'll be glad you did.

God's View of Prosperity

God wants to meet your every need: spirit, soul, and body.

God's person and nature is clearly revealed in His dealings with His people throughout history. His goodness is progressively revealed to us in our need and shortcomings.

For example, He desires that we come into our own Promised Land of provision and protection. God promised Israel a land of abundance where they would experience no lack. This land of milk and honey was His will for the Old Testament people of God. Today, His will is still to bless his New Testament people, the church. Wherever the people of God now live, that land is blessed because God is there in the midst of His people. He directed them there, helped them to get there, and established them in it. More particularly, the land in modern terms may be defined as our sphere of endeavor: our own business or the job we hold. It is not merely a spiritual state of being, but includes our needs being met in the material realm.

> For the LORD your God is bringing you into a good land, a land of brooks of water, of fountains and springs, that flow out of valleys and hills; a land of wheat and barley, of vines and fig trees and pomegranates, a land of olive oil and honey; a land in which you will eat bread without scarcity, in which you will lack nothing.
>
> Deuteronomy 8:7–9

God wants to bless us daily with a load of benefits. The Father's nature is to give us all things that we need for life and godliness (2 Peter 1:3). He is by nature a giver, not a taker. He so loved us that He gave His son Jesus so that we might be saved and His blessing and provision would rest upon us on a daily basis.

> Blessed be the Lord, who daily loads us with benefits.
>
> Psalm 68:19

He delights to see His children do well. Why? First, He loves us, and second, our prosperity is a witness and testimony to His goodness. We bring Him glory when we do well. As we favor or play our part in advancing God's kingdom, we can shout for joy, knowing that God is for us, not against us.

> Let them shout for joy and be glad,
> Who favor my righteous cause;
> And let them say continually,
> "Let the Lord be magnified,
> Who has pleasure in the prosperity of his servant."

> Psalm 35:27

What a generous and caring heavenly Father we have. He loves us and entered into covenant with us through Jesus in such a way that even our material needs are taken care of. We are instructed to say continually that the Lord is to be magnified and that His pleasure or delight is in our prosperity. Faith finds its first expression in saying or confessing the will of God. Faith does not speak out what the current circumstances may be; rather, it boldly declares God's will or intent, which is our prosperity or well–being: spirit, soul and body.

We can also see from the above verse that we are to favor His righteous cause. The spreading of the gospel of salvation in Christ is God's righteous cause. When we play our part in supporting the work of the gospel, we favor what God is doing on the earth, and He continues to pour His blessing on us. There is a continual flow of blessing from God to us and then to others in need. The Christian who does not want to be blessed is damming up the flow. Scripture encourages us to be generous and large hearted toward the needy. Why tighten up, and with a false humility rooted in ignorance, refuse to receive the blessings of God, which can be passed on to others in a spirit of generosity?

Be sure to watch what you say about God's will concerning prosperity. Do not be bound by some religious nonsense that has no scriptural foundation. Glorify God in both the words you speak and the deeds you do. When you continually say that God delights in your prosperity, you come into agreement with His will and play your part in connecting with God's provision in the spirit.

Promised Prosperity

God has promised to provide for you.

God provides for us by means of His promises. When we know, understand, believe, and declare His promises in our lives, we access, or receive, God's supply. Consider the promise made to the Philippians who had participated in the spreading of the gospel: 'And my God shall supply all your need according to his riches in glory by Christ Jesus' (Philippians 4:19). They had played their part in practically supporting Paul's ministry. In return, they could then claim the promise of God's provision. He would meet their needs according to his riches.

There is always a divine exchange with God. When we interact with Him in furthering His purposes through ministry, we can expect to enjoy the benefit of His promises. When we release what is in our hand, God has promised to release the riches that are in His hand or under His control.

Consider the example of the promises God made to the children of Israel. He laid out His promises before the Israelites actually entered their land. A promise always comes before the fact. That's where faith starts. Promises are given with responsibilities to fulfill. The promises were conditional. All promises are! If you do this, then you enjoy that! It really is that simple in God's economy. This is not works but a faith response to His grace.

> Now it shall come to pass, if you diligently obey the voice of the LORD your God, to observe carefully all his commandments which I command you today, that the LORD your God will set you high above all nations of the earth. And all these blessings shall come upon you and overtake you, because you obey the voice of the LORD your God.
>
> Deuteronomy 28:1–2

God goes on to describe in verses 3 through 13 all the promised material blessings that result from obedience. The blessings cover all aspects of life: where you live, what you do, and protection from danger; even your animals will be blessed. There will be so much substance that there will be enough to lend to other nations.

Some have argued that God blessed the Old Testament Israelites with material blessings, but today He blesses New Testament believers with spiritual blessings. Scripture teaches that both Old and New Testament believers were blessed in all spheres of life: spiritual and physical, or material. The Old Testament believers had the covenant of forgiveness, were called as a holy nation of priests to God himself. They were blessed spiritually above all nations as a witness to the world of God's covenant favor. Yet they were also blessed materially for their obedience.

Coming on over to the New Testament, it is clear that we who are now in Christ Jesus are blessed with all spiritual blessings (Ephesians 1:3). However, the Word goes on to reveal that God has also provided for our material well–being (2 Corinthians 8:9). Jesus was made to be poor so that we might enjoy a full supply or be made rich. Check it out for yourself. The context of this passage concerns material matters. Jesus was able to amply supply His disciples and a whole lot more for three years of largely traveling ministry. He did it through the faithful support of people who gave generously into His ministry.

God is the God of more than enough. His children ought to reflect His nature, yet many Christians are not in a position to lend to others. Many are standing in line for handouts themselves! This should not be so.

Could it be that by and large Christians are either ignorant of or disobedient to God's commandments concerning prosperity? Prosperity is promised in the Word, but to walk in the benefits, we have the responsibility to obey and walk in God's ways. Let us now look at God's ways concerning prosperity.

One of the spiritual laws that unlock God's promised provision is the law of sowing and reaping. The law states that whatever a person sows, that will he reap.

> Do not be deceived, God is not mocked; for whatever a man sows, that he will also reap.
>
> Galatians 6:7

> While the earth remains, seedtime and harvest, cold and heat, winter and summer, and day and night shall not cease.
>
> Genesis 8:22

In order to reap a harvest, you have to sow seed in a field. Ask any farmer whether sitting on his porch watching an empty field will bring him a rich harvest. No, he has to get out there with seed and plant the crop. He then has to tend to that crop, water or irrigate it. Then, and only then, can he expect a harvest. He even has to know how and when to reap the harvest. There is no use in the framer praying for a harvest or even fasting for a harvest. He must sow in order to reap.

In the area of material provision, the same applies. We cannot expect God to bless us materially without sowing seed. That means playing our part in giving to the gospel through tithes and offerings.

God has promised to give to the one who sows both bread to eat (current needs) and also seed to sow for the next crop (future growth). In our modern context, seed represents finances or money. We need both money to live on (bread to eat), and money to sow. If we purpose to obey God and sow financial seed, He will see to it that we have both the seed to continue to sow and the necessary supply to meet our needs.

> Now may he who supplies seed to the sower, and bread for food, supply and multiply the seed you have sown and increase the fruits of your righteousness.
>
> 2 Corinthians 9:10

When we play our part and sow seed, God then plays His part and multiplies the seed and causes increase. Both the spiritual and material realms are naturally geared up for increase. God is the God of increase and he created all things. The crop that is reaped from sowing seed is always far, far greater than the actual seed sown. One bag of seed can produce a harvest way beyond that bag's original content.

The mechanism for increase is sowing. Wishful thinking about God's goodness is not going to produce a harvest. Sowing is. As we have seen, we should say that God delights in our prosperity, but we follow through with corresponding actions and sow seed to produce a harvest.

Personally, we have experienced financial increase when we have sown seed money into other people's lives and ministries while believing God's promise to increase our own fruits. We released our faith as we sowed by declaring out loud in prayer what we expected from God on the basis of His promised blessing.

Finances from unusual and surprising sources have been released to us on many occasions. The seed we sowed was multiplied back to us! Some may say this is a mercenary approach to giving. We prefer to think of it as obedience to God's ways. He says to do it, we obey, and the means by which our loving Heavenly Father God blesses us are then opened up.

Why Prosper?

God blesses you because He loves you and so that you can be a channel of blessing to others.

In a world dominated by fear and greed, it is encouraging to know that God is not reactionary. He has always sought to bless His chosen people so that they could be conduits of blessing to those in need. His people become His instruments of righteousness. When Abraham was called to be a nation builder, God laid the foundation. He would bless all the families of the earth through him. Put simply, Abraham was to be blessed in order to be a blessing to others. He was not to consume the blessing all on himself, but rather to be a channel of God's goodness to others.

> I will make you a great nation;
> I will bless you and make your name great;
> And you shall be a blessing.
> I will bless those who bless you,
> And I will curse him who curses you;

> And in you all the families of the earth shall be
> blessed.

> Genesis 12:2–3

Today, through Christ (Abraham's Seed), we become the channel of blessing to the world in both word and deed. Generosity is a virtue and characteristic of God. We accurately portray that character of God when we give and bless. When we are reluctant to give and withhold more than we should, we devalue God in the eyes of the world. Our goal is to lift up His name, not trample it through stinginess born from ignorance, fear and greed.

Let's not be confused. Jesus came to alleviate man's ills. He lived, died, and rose again so that we could be free from sin, sickness, and lack. As His representatives, we are to play our part in extending God's grace to people in need. How can we do this if we ourselves are bound by sin, sickness, and lack? We have to be blessed in order to be a blessing.

If wealth and abundance draw you away from the things of God, then you have a heart problem, not a money problem. If you establish your heart in God and learn to be content whether you have or have not, then God can trust you with His abundance. You can become a vessel through which He can pour out His blessings to others. The key issue is whether you see your wealth glorifying God or self. If Jesus is Lord over your finances, then there should be no problem. Your will has been submitted to His.

Receive Your Prosperity

God has given His word to bless us. If we respond and obey His principles, we will enjoy His promised provision that caters to the needs of our whole being: spirit, soul, and body. Prosperity is a gift given by God, but we must receive it by faith.

As we learn to avoid evil and delight in God's law as a lifestyle, we are compared to a tree planted by rivers of water. As a loving Father God will honor our obedience and faithfulness with His promised prosperity. We will receive in due season everything He has promised.

> Blessed is the man
> Who walks not in the counsel of the ungodly,
> Nor stands in the path of sinners,
> Nor sits in the seat of the scornful;
> But his delight is in the law of the LORD,
> And in his law he meditates day and night.
> He shall be like a tree
> Planted by the rivers of water,

That brings forth its fruit in its season,
Whose leaf also shall not wither;
And whatever he does shall prosper.

Psalm 1:1–3

Of course, we have to play our part by doing what we do with our whole heart, mind, and strength. God blesses the work of our hands, not the seat of our pants. As we go about our business or life's work, we are to expect God to bless us. Faith expects God to live up to His promises, and as we ask God for good things, our expectation becomes His invitation to honor His Word and bless us!

If you then, being evil, know how to give good gifts to your children, how much more will your Father who is in heaven give good things to those who ask him!

Matthew 7:11

God's grace is always accessed by faith. Faith asks for what God has promised in His covenant. Asking is neither presumptuous nor arrogant. Rather, it is required by God. That is the way of doing things in His kingdom. You have not because you ask not. When you ask, be sure to do so in faith, and declare out loud what you believe. Base it on a firm promise.

Study the Word, know the promises, and then ask in faith.

> For assuredly, I say to you, whoever says to this mountain, "Be removed and be cast into the sea," and does not doubt in his heart, but believes that those things he says will come to pass, he will have whatever he says. Therefore I say to you, whatever things you ask when you pray, believe that you receive them, and you will have them.
>
> Mark 11:23–24

In order to receive you have to actively ask God in prayer for the things you know He wants to give you. Your faith begins where you know the will of God personally. You cannot pray in faith when you are guessing what His will is. You can only approach God on the basis of what you know is His will, and we have seen that it is His will to bless us so that we can be a blessing to others.

Be sure to match your faith requests to God with corresponding obedience and action. Faith is proactive, not passive, and in order to reap, we must keep on sowing.

> Give, and it will be given to you: good measure, pressed down, shaken together, and running over will be put into your bosom. For with the same

measure that you use, it will be measured back
to you.

Luke 6:38

Another wonderful passage underlines this truth
so clearly.

There is one who scatters, yet increases more;
And there is one who withholds more than is
right,
But it leads to poverty.
The generous soul will be made rich,
And he who waters will also be watered himself.
The people will curse him who withholds grain,
But blessing will be on the head of him who sells it.

Proverbs 11:24–26

Another key principle in giving is the measure and
intent of our giving. Our giving must be planned, not
haphazard or without definite intent or purpose. We
must also be cheerful and generous in our giving.

Therefore I thought it necessary to exhort the
brethren to go to you ahead of time, and prepare your generous gift beforehand, which you
had previously promised, that it may be ready
as a matter of generosity and not as a grudging
obligation. But this I say: He who sows sparingly
will also reap sparingly, and he who sows boun-

tifully will also reap bountifully. So let each one give as he purposes in his heart, not grudgingly or of necessity; for God loves a cheerful giver.

2 Corinthians 9:5–7

Giving ought to be a matter of the heart and not because someone cleverly plays on your emotions or uses high pressure tactics. God loves a cheerful giver, not a tearful one who gives reluctantly and under compulsion, later to regret their decision to give.

Pitfalls to Avoid

As our loving Father, God warns us of the pitfalls associated with money matters. It is vital to have and maintain an unhindered relationship with God. If the pursuit of material possessions hinders our relationship with God, then we need to be honest about our motives. God gives us His Word, His Spirit and fellow believers to which we are accountable to help us be honest. Our true motives must be separated from self–deception, a condition quite common to human nature.

In short, we are instructed not to let the cares of this world and the deceitfulness of riches choke the Word or hinder our relationship with God.

> Now these are the ones sown among thorns; they are the ones who hear the word, and the cares of this world, the deceitfulness of riches, and the desires for other things entering in choke the word, and it becomes unfruitful.
>
> Mark 4:18–19

Ordinary cares of this world are in themselves not sinful. Only when they distract us from a vital relationship with God do they then choke the Word already in our hearts. It is a matter of priority. When we worry about how to solve the cares of life, we are tempted to turn our attention to setting things straight ourselves. We work harder, and the cares start to dominate our time and emotional energy. Slowly, the life begins to drain out of our relationship with God as we struggle on our own.

On the other hand, when things are going well and we now have a little more time and money to spare, a natural tendency is to be deceived into thinking that our efforts and struggle needs to be rewarded with time off! We relax, and if we are not careful, we do not press into the things of God because the things of this world now capture our attention.

Let me illustrate. There was a guy who was struggling to make ends meet who decided to go to his pastor for prayer, counsel, and support. His relationship with God had suffered as he struggled to deal with the cares he was facing. After seeing the pastor, he made an effort to get back into fellowship with God and his fellow churchgoers. Things began to turn around. He was now praying and worshiping God regularly, and the Lord blessed his efforts and things freed up so much that he was able to get a boat and spend quality family time doing fun stuff out on the lake on week-ends. The only problem was that the family started to skip Sundays to enjoy even more quality time together. Then the boat had to be cleaned, repaired, painted, and new equipment installed. Slowly the time he had left for God got less and less, and the cares of keeping things up started to choke his relationship with God again. Soon he was back to square one with all the problems that had crept in maintaining matters at this new level.

God knows us better than we know ourselves, and warns us that we are not to forget Him when things go well. The love of money is the root of all sorts of evil. Money itself is neutral, but when our love shifts from God to money, that is the beginning of trouble.

Then when success comes, we have to watch its influence. Most often success is more difficult to handle than failure, even when the blessing or success comes from God!

> When you have eaten and are full, then you shall bless the LORD your God for the good land which He has given you. Beware that you do not forget the LORD your God by not keeping his commandments, His judgments, and His statutes which I command you today.
>
> Deuteronomy 8:10–11

Later on in this passage, we are instructed to remember God as the source of blessing and that His blessing is for the purpose of establishing His covenant. If we settle these matters in our heart, we will not be drawn away by success and prosperity but honor God with it.

> And you shall remember the LORD your God, for it is he who gives you power to get wealth, that he may establish his covenant which he swore to your fathers, as it is this day.
>
> Deuteronomy 8:18

Life is lived from the heart, so be sure to take time to examine your motives. You can't fool God, so don't waste time fooling yourself or others. Be sure to keep your motives pure. Impure motives have a habit of being exposed. If we lust after pleasure, problems will arise. If we hunger and seek after God and have our priorities right, then pleasure will find its proper place. God will be our source and supplier. We will avoid covetousness and strife and honor Him with our prosperity.

> Where do wars and fights come from among you? Do they not come from your desires for pleasure that war in your members? You lust and do not have. You murder and covet and cannot obtain.

Edmund Horak

You fight and war. Yet you do not have because you do not ask. You ask and do not receive, because you ask amiss, that you may spend it on your pleasures.

James 4:1–3

Be Practical

God has always looked for people who respond to him in faith. His sovereignty is accessed by faith. It does not operate in a vacuum. It is by grace through faith that we are saved. God initiates, we respond in faith, and the transaction becomes complete.

> For by grace you have been saved through faith, and that not of yourselves; it is the gift of God, not of works, lest anyone should boast. For we are his workmanship, created in Christ Jesus for good works, which God prepared beforehand that we should walk in them.
>
> Ephesians 2:8–10

His grace is attached to His purposes. He has good works prepared for each one of us to fulfill, and we need an abundance of supply for these good works. This supply is received by faith. If things just fell in our lap because God willed it, how come so many

Christians are sitting waiting with empty laps? Faith is a force that must be used to connect earth's need with heaven's supply.

God's promises are appropriated by faith. God made a covenant with us through Jesus, and in Him all the promises are yes and amen. In fact, heaven is full of promises waiting for us to claim by faith. We possess the promises by what we say and do! Faith has a voice, and the redeemed must say so!

> Oh, give thanks to the LORD, for he is good!
> For his mercy endures forever.
> Let the redeemed of the LORD say so.
>
> Psalm 107:2

When we praise God for what He has already done for us through Jesus and boldly declare that we are redeemed from sin, sickness and poverty, God has promised to watch over his Word to perform it in our lives. He is bound by his Word to do what He has promised. He has promised to supply our every need and even to give us the desires of our hearts. When we speak his Word over our lives, things are set in motion in the spirit realm that eventually play out in the natural affairs of life.

Faith must be exercised in every area of life. God cares about our work and wants to favor us in what we put our hands to.

His favor is attached to His wisdom. As we value and ask for wisdom, listen to His voice; He will guide us in the affairs of daily life. Know that God can and does bless you by a variety of means. Be open to any and all of them. Some examples are:

- Your own labor: jobs and better jobs
- Gifts given by others
- Raises and bonuses
- New opportunities
- Estates and inheritances
- Debt cancellation

These are all ways in which God's favor can be manifest as we walk by faith and expect Him to honor His promises to bless us. Remember, God's favor is always His gift to us and unmerited. We receive His favor by grace through our faith and not because of some inherent self–righteousness.

It is important to obey God in the area of tithes and offerings. A tithe is ten percent of all income, and offerings are anything over and above that. The tithe belongs to God, and He leaves us to live on the remaining ninety percent, which He blesses.

When the tithe is given to God, His Word teaches that the windows of heaven are opened up above us. In Bible days, this referred to the blessings of ample rain for the crops to grow. When the rain fell and the crops grew, the people of God enjoyed abundance. In times of drought, there were obvious problems.

Today, in our modern context, we still ultimately rely on God's provision in this way, but for the city dweller, the blessing and favor of God comes through such areas as jobs, sales, commissions, contracts, raises, bonuses, etc.

When you give your tithe to God, consecrate it to God and ask Him to open up opportunities of increase in your daily life.

> "Bring all the tithes into the storehouse,
> That there may be food in My house,
> And try Me now in this,"
> Says the LORD of hosts,
> "If I will not open for you the windows of heaven
> And pour out for you such blessing
> That there will not be room enough to receive it."
>
> Malachi 3:10

In summary, be practical! Declare God's promises of prosperity out loud, put your hand to something practical, and be sure to willingly give God the tithe and, in addition, offerings. He will honor your consistent and committed obedience to his financial plan.

How to Deal with Debt

Debt hinders us from being able to give to others.

To be financially indebted to individuals and institutions that charge exorbitant interest is not God's best. Sure, some may be able to juggle their debt in such a way to set up and maintain a certain acceptable lifestyle, but many cannot. They are, as the Bible puts it, enslaved to debt.

> The rich rules over the poor,
> And the borrower is servant to the lender.
>
> Proverbs 22:7

The Bible also teaches that God alone is to be our ruler. When another man rules us through financial means, we resent that situation. Resentment is not good as it drains us of life. We should be free to enjoy the earth and its resources and not be in a continual state of bondage, whether it be mental, emotional or financial. We are supposed to serve one another with love, not be in bondage to one another through finances.

The world system of borrowing and lending at high interest is designed to make the rich richer and the poor poorer. If you are rich that may seem fine, but the overall mix of things is not pleasing to God, who has placed us in a world that has enough to go around if there were no greed and usury (excessive interest). In God's economy, it is not a good thing for one man to get rich at another's expense. Christians should be living their lives in such a way that they please God and bless mankind.

God wants us to come into a land of more than enough, where our needs and even our sanctified desires are met. This land is a place of financial freedom where we lift our heads up from the proverbial 'grindstone' and see the needs of others less fortunate than ourselves. We are able to give to those in need. We even have time to not only give them a fish, but also teach them how to fish for themselves or make their own way in life. We should engage with them in such a way as to give them the wisdom of God for their situation. This state of blessedness moves us from self to serving and furthers the kingdom of God among men.

It remains more blessed to give than to receive: "And remember the words of the Lord Jesus, that he said, 'It is more blessed to give than to receive'" (Acts 20:35).

Some steps to take in the journey to freedom from debt:

- Soberly evaluate your lifestyle and spending habits in the light of the Word.

- Say no to unnecessary spending. Hard as it may be, saying no to things that bring temporary meaning and satisfaction sets us free to enjoy things that really count. Set a spending budget.

- Seek specific financial counsel on strategic steps to take to get out of debt. Diligence and planning produce plenty: 'The plans of the diligent lead surely to plenty, but those of everyone who is hasty, surely to poverty' (Proverbs 21:5).

- Establish a giving account, and plan your giving with specific, measurable giving goals according to the principles of God's Word outlined here. This usually goes against the natural tendency to hold onto what you've got because it's needed. For the supernatural favor of God to flow into your life, you have to keep on giving as a lifestyle.

- Pay back debt with the extra funds now available. Start with the smaller debts. When these are paid off, they will provide you with momentum to tackle the larger ones. Be wise with any debt consolidation schemes, which often simply stretch out the payments over a longer time. They are often based on the equity of your home if you own one, and you should always protect your home.

Realize that through faith, patience, and diligent obedient application of the Word, debt can be broken. Give God enough time to help you make more and spend less as debt is reduced. Keep your relationship with God your central focus, seek His kingdom first, and watch how He takes care of the matters you have been so worried about. Cast your cares upon Him, put His Word into practice, attend and get involved in a local church, serve others, pray, worship, witness, and above all walk in the faith, hope and love of God. Peace will be your constant companion.

God's Financial Program

Prospering God's way involves both doing and saying.

Prosperity has a process. It is not magical—that 'poof' something happens out of nowhere and suddenly we are prosperous. There are no get–rich–quick schemes in the Word of God. God has instructed us to understand and follow His ways through his Word. God will supply the grace, something that only He can do. We respond to Him in faith. God does not need faith. We do. A faith response involves corresponding actions. If we are convinced that God delights in our prosperity, then we must put feet to our faith and follow through with God's program. The underlying principle in the following financial program is seedtime and harvest. You sow seeds and you reap a harvest.

First, give your tithes (a tenth of income, our first fruits) to the local storehouse or church where you are planted or in relationship with. Be sure to be obedient to God's plan of regular fellowship and involvement in the local church.

Bring all the tithes into the storehouse.

Malachi 3:8

And all the tithe of the land, whether of the seed of the land or of the fruit of the tree, is the LORD's. It is holy to the LORD.

Leviticus 27: 30–33

Honor the LORD with your possessions,
And with the firstfruits of all your increase;
So your barns will be filled with plenty,
And your vats will overflow with new wine.

Proverbs 3:9–10

Second, give offerings (over and above the tithe) to both the local church and other ministries as the Lord directs.

Give, and it will be given to you: good measure, pressed down, shaken together, and running over will be put into your bosom. For with the same measure that you use, it will be measured back to you.

Luke 6:38

Now the multitude of those who believed were of one heart and one soul; neither did anyone say that any of the things he possessed was his

own, but they had all things in common. And
with great power the apostles gave witness to the
resurrection of the Lord Jesus. And great grace
was upon them all. Nor was there anyone among
them who lacked; for all who were possessors of
lands or houses sold them, and brought the pro-
ceeds of the things that were sold, and laid them
at the apostles' feet; and they distributed to each
as anyone had need.

Acts 4:32–37

Third, minister to the poor in whatever way you
can as the Lord directs. Find someone less fortunate
than you. Be open and sensitive to the promptings of
the Holy Spirit and any opportunities that arise. Give
away clothing, goods, food, and even cash where you
are led to. Be a blessing even when they do not deserve
it. All of us never deserved to be saved anyway, so
what's new? Be gracious like God!

He who has pity on the poor lends to the LORD,
And he will pay back what he has given.

Proverbs 19:17

Fourth, support traveling and other missionaries
that minister to people who reach out to parts of the
world you cannot go to. Once again, this support should
come after your local church tithes and offerings.

Now you Philippians know also that in the beginning of the gospel, when I departed from Macedonia, no church shared with me concerning giving and receiving but you only. For even in Thessalonica you sent aid once and again for my necessities. Not that I seek the gift, but I seek the fruit that abounds to your account. Indeed I have all and abound. I am full, having received from Epaphroditus the things sent from you, a sweet–smelling aroma, an acceptable sacrifice, well pleasing to God. And my God shall supply all your need according to his riches in glory by Christ Jesus.

Philippians 4:15–16

Paul was a traveling minister that received his financial support from willing saints who gave to his ministry over and above their local commitments. He certainly wasn't financed by the local mafia, but by people who identified with God's greater purposes in the universal body of Christ. Today, there are ministries that travel worldwide in areas that you and I may not be able to directly reach, but through these other ministries we can participate in reaching them indirectly. God will put these good works to our shared account. Sow into the good soil of ministries you trust and identify with for their integrity and fruitfulness.

Fifth, give to your brothers in Christ that are in need. Resist the temptation to think of yourself as the only one in need. There are other Christians in need. Be open to give to them and see how God will take care of you. This is His way of doing things. He wants to create a flow of blessing in the body of Christ. From me to you to another and so on, like a flowing river.

> Now all who believed were together, and had all things in common, and sold their possessions and goods, and divided them among all, as anyone had need.
>
> Acts 2:44–45

Open your heart to your brothers in need. Let the love of God flow out of your heart in real and practical ways, not merely in word only.

> By this we know love, because he laid down his life for us. And we also ought to lay down our lives for the brethren. But whoever has this world's goods, and sees his brother in need, and shuts up his heart from him, how does the love of God abide in him? My little children, let us not love in word or in tongue, but in deed and in truth.
>
> 1 John 3:16–18

When we look at all the above avenues for giving, it should motivate us to trust God and order our lives and spending in such a way that we break out beyond simple survival from one paycheck to the next. God wants us to prosper to establish His covenant, not to consume it all on month–to–month spending and self-ish pursuits. It is my conviction that when someone sees by faith the eternal value of reaching people with their prosperity, he or she will pay the price and give sacrificially, as well as from his or her abundance.

It is wonderful and blessed to receive, but it is more so to give. Jesus said so.

Possess Your Prosperity

To review, when you walk in obedience to God's principles and practices (are doers of the Word), you can confidently claim His promised provision with a thankful and worshipful heart.

> Let them say continually, let the Lord be magnified, Who has pleasure in the prosperity of his servant.
>
> Psalm 35:27

The first act of faith is saying what God says about you. You are required to agree with God by stating the terms of your covenant. Faith requires an active response to God's promises. It is not passively wishing in your mind that God would move, but boldly declaring that He is already moving on your behalf to establish His covenant in your life.

Of course, as we have seen, you must follow through with practical steps by putting your hand to some endeavor. You cannot merely sit on your "blessed assurance" and do nothing. God blesses the work of your hands, not the seat of your pants. Yet the spirit or heart essence of faith is to speak out that which you believe (2 Corinthians 4:13). The following affirmations of faith will chart your course toward God's will for your life concerning material well–being or prosperity. Boldly and regularly declare out loud these Scripture–based affirmations; meaning them from a heart yielded to the integrity of God's Word. You might even want to say them over and over again till the meaning and significance really settles down into your heart. Your faith is fed as your hear the Word of God spoken, not only by others as they preach and teach, but also by your own mouth!

- "Lord, I come before you with a thankful and grateful heart for your heart of generous pro-vision. You take pleasure in my prosperity and well–being: spirit, soul, and body. You supply all my needs according to your wonderful riches in glory.

- "My delight is in You and Your purposes for my life. I set my affections on things above and avoid covetousness. I chose to establish your kingdom by obeying Your Word concerning a lifestyle of giving. I give cheerfully and generously of my tithes and offerings whilst supporting those in need (my brothers and the poor). Your grace (or ability in my life) enables me to have abundance for every good work.

- "I know and believe that You have promised to open up the windows of heaven, or practical opportunities, to me so that I might prosper. I am diligent at my work and plan my financial affairs with Your wisdom. In faith I declare that the work of my hands is prospering.

- "My heart is to worship and honor You not only in spirit and in truth but with my substance too."

Back up your words with corresponding actions! Become a consistent doer of the Word by setting in motion the financial program outlined in the previous chapter. You can only expect God to do His part when you do yours.

May you be blessed as you cooperate with God in establishing His covenant of prosperity in your life.

Tithes and Offerings

Bring all the tithes into the storehouse,
That there may be food in My house,
And try Me now in this,"
Says the LORD of hosts,
"If I will not open for you the windows of heaven
And pour out for you such blessing
That there will not be room enough to receive it.
"And I will rebuke the devourer for your sakes,
So that he will not destroy the fruit of your ground,
Nor shall the vine fail to bear fruit for you in the
field,"
Says the LORD of hosts.

Malachi 3:10–11

Speak to the children of Israel, that they bring
Me an offering. From everyone who gives it willingly with his heart you shall take My offering.

Exodus 25:2

What Is the Tithe?

- The first tenth (ten percent) of all increase.

Exodus 23:19

What Is an Offering?

- Offerings are anything above and beyond the tithe.

Luke 6:38

- Old Testament: offerings generally given for buildings—tabernacles, temples, wall construction, etc.

Exodus 35:21

- New Testament: the early church support included:

Their own needy
Acts 2:40–47

General ministry
Acts 4:32–37

Famine relief
Acts 11:27–30

Missionary work
Philippians 4:19

Why Should I Tithe?

- God commands it: "Bring all the tithes…"

  Malachi 3:10

- To support ministers who serve you.

  Leviticus 27:30

- You protect the remaining ninety percent.

  Proverbs 3:9

Where Should I Tithe?

- To your local church storehouse.

  Malachi 3:10

- Support for TV ministries, evangelists, and traveling ministers are offerings above the tithe.

  Philippians 4:19

Isn't It My Money Anyway?

- God, as creator, owns it all.

  Psalm 24:1

- All that we have (life, time, talents, possessions and finances) is given to us by God.

  Psalm 115:16

Why do some struggle with giving their tithes and offerings?

- Ignorance: not adequately taught.

Hosea 4:6

- Disobedience: selfish tendencies.

Deuteronomy 28:15

- Bad experiences in the past.

Ezekiel 22:27

Does God Promise to Bless Me When I Give?

- Our obedience is rewarded.

Deuteronomy 28:1

- Giving opens up God's blessings.

Luke 6:38

How Do I Give?

- Speak faith and worship God.

Deuteronomy 26:5–10

- Give systematically, not haphazardly.

1 Corinthians 16:1–4

- Give according to your ability.

2 Corinthians 8:3, 13

- Be generous and give cheerfully.

2 Corinthians 9:6–7

- Praise God for the promised increase.

Psalm 66:5–7

- Give with an attitude of worship.

1 Chronicles 16:29

- Remembrance of God's enablement.

Deuteronomy 8:18

What Kind of Church Can You Trust to Support?

It is important to confidently identify with the church you attend and support financially. If someone has misgivings about the church's finances, he or she will be reluctant to fully get behind the leadership and vision of the church. Some people will always be difficult to please, but most will develop confidence in a church that:

- Reaches out to the community.

Acts 2:40–47

- Takes care of its own needy.

Acts 4:32–35

- Takes care of its leadership.

1 Timothy 5:17–18

- Is transparent about finances.

1 Corinthians 4:2

Additional Scriptures by Topic

(For the development of your own 'Money Moments' in the future).

You might want to create your own 'Money Moment' using the following references, or go through them in your own devotions. They could also be broken up into their topics and given as a weekly devotional outline in the church bulletin or on the website. A heading like this could be used: 'What the Bible says about...' followed by the topic heading and the scripture references. If you do something like this, then get your graphics people to create a visually appealing and easily identifiable heading that brands this part of the website or bulletin.

Budgeting:
Proverbs 6:6–8
Proverbs 21:5
Proverbs 22:3
Proverbs 24:3–4
Proverbs 25:28
Proverbs 27:12
Proverbs 27:23
Luke 14:28–30
1 Corinthians 16:2

Contentment:
Ecclesiastes 5:10
Luke 3:14
Luke 12:15
Philippians 4:11–13
Colossians 3:15
1 Timothy 6:6–10
Hebrews 13:5

Co-signing:
Psalm 37:26
Proverbs 6:1–2
Proverbs 11:15
Proverbs 17:18
Proverbs 22:26–27
Proverbs 27:13

Debt:
Deuteronomy 15:6
Deuteronomy 28:12
Psalm 37:21
Proverbs 22:7
Proverbs 22:26–27
Ecclesiastes 5:5
Romans 13:8

Giving:
Deuteronomy 14:23
Deuteronomy 15:10
Proverbs 3:9–10
Proverbs 11:25
Proverbs 22:9
Matthew 23:23
Luke 6:38
Acts 20:35
1 Corinthians 16:1–2
2 Corinthians 8: 13–14
2 Corinthians 9:6–8
Hebrews 7:1–2

Our needs met:
1 Chronicles 28:20
Psalm 37:25
Matthew 6:31–32

Matthew 7:11
Luke 12:7
John 21:6
2 Corinthians 9:8
Philippians 4:19

Investing:
Proverbs 15:22
Proverbs 24:27
Proverbs 28:20
Ecclesiastes 11:2
Matthew 25:14–26

Lending:
Exodus 22:25
Deuteronomy 23:19–20
Leviticus 25:35–37
Proverbs 3:27–28
Proverbs 28:8
Matthew 5:42

Planning:
Genesis 41:34–36
Proverbs 6:6–8
Proverbs 15:22
Proverb 16:9
Proverbs 21:5

Proverbs 22:3
Proverbs 24:3–4
Proverbs 24:27
Ecclesiastes 11:2
Luke 14:28–30
1 Corinthians 16:1–2

Priorities:
Exodus 23:12
Matthew 6:21
Matthew 6:24
Matthew 6:33

Prosperity:
Genesis 39:3
Joshua 1:8
1 Chronicles 22:12
2 Chronicles 31:21
Psalm 1: 1–3
Psalm 37:4
Proverbs 10:22
Malachi 3:10
Matthew 6:4
Matthew 19:29
Ephesians 3:20
3 John 1:2

Saving:

Proverbs 21:5
Proverbs 21:20
Proverbs 27:12
Proverbs 30:24–25
1 Corinthians 16:2

Stewardship:

Exodus 35:35
Deuteronomy 10:14
I Chronicles 29:11
Psalm 50:10–12
Luke 3:11
Luke 6:30
Luke 12:47–48
Luke 14:33
Luke 16:9–11
Romans 14:8

Success:

Joshua 1:8
Psalm 1:1–3
Psalm 37:4
Proverbs 22:4
Proverbs 22:29
Matthew 23:12
Luke 9:48

Ephesians 3:20

Taxes:

Matthew 22:21
Romans 13:7

Tithing:

Genesis 28:20–22
Exodus 23:19
Proverbs 3:9–10
Proverbs 11:24–25
Ezekiel 44:30
Malachi 3:8–10
Matthew 23:23
Luke 12:33–34
2 Corinthians 9:7
Galatians 6:7
Hebrews 7:1–10

Work:

Genesis 2:15
Exodus 23:12
2 Chronicles 31:21
Nehemiah 4:6
Proverbs 10:4
Proverbs 12:24
Proverbs 13:4

Proverbs 14:23
Proverbs 18:9
Proverbs 22:29
Proverbs 24:27
Proverbs 28:19
Ecclesiastes 5:12
Ecclesiastes 9:10
Daniel 6:3
Matthew 5:41
Colossians 3:17
Colossians 3:23
2 Thessalonians 3:10–11
1 Timothy 5:8

SECTION F

On the Lighter Side

These examples of humor could be used to lighten up (but not trivialize) the atmosphere when the "Money Moment" is given during a service. These could also be used in a bulletin or Web site.

- The nicest thing about money is that it never clashes with anything I wear.

- The only time a nickel goes as far as it once did is when it rolls under a bed.

- Few people can stand prosperity, especially the other fellow's.

- We are living in an unprecedented era of prosperity. Never before have so many acquired so much unpaid–for stuff!

- Give God what's right, not what's left.

- Sign at Car Dealership: "Best way to get back on your feet: miss a payment."

- Give Satan an inch in your finances and he'll be a ruler in no time.

- It is unlikely there'll be a reduction in the wages of sin.

- A little boy in church for the first time watched as the ushers passed around the offering plates. When they came near his pew, the boy said loudly, "Don't pay for me Daddy. I'm under five."

- Did you know that the size of a dollar bill can change? It's small when you go buy a car, but huge when you place it in the offering!

- A lady at work was seen putting a credit card into her floppy drive and pulling it out very quickly. When I inquired as to what she was doing, she said she was shopping on the Internet and they kept asking for a credit card number, so she was using the ATM "thingy."

- New Building Program:
  There is the story of a pastor who got up one Sunday and announced to his congregation, "I have good news and bad news. The good news is we have enough money to pay for our new building program. The bad news is it's still out there in your pockets.

- A Choice of Hymns:
One Sunday, a pastor told his congregation that the church needed some extra money and asked the people to prayerfully consider giving a little extra in the offering plate. He said that whoever gave the most would be able to pick out three hymns. After the offering plates were passed, the pastor glanced down and noticed that someone had placed a one–thousand–dollar bill in offering. He was so excited that he immediately shared his joy with his congregation and said he'd like to personally thank the person who placed the money in the plate. A very quiet, elderly, saintly lady all the way in the back shyly raised her hand. The pastor asked her to come to the front. Slowly, she made her way to the pastor. He told her how wonderful it was that she gave so much and in thanksgiving asked her to pick out three hymns. Her eyes brightened as she looked over the congregation, pointed to the three handsomest men in the building and said, "I'll take him and him and him."

- Dear Pastor,
I liked your sermon where you said that good health is more important than money, but I still want a raise in my allowance. Sincerely, Eleanor, age 12.

- Dear Pastor,
  I'm sorry I can't leave more money in the plate, but my father didn't give me a raise in my allowance. Could you have a sermon about a raise in my allowance? Love, Patty, age 10.

- Groom–to–be:
  The prospective father–in–law asked, "Young man, can you support a family?" The surprised groom–to–be replied, "Well, no. I was just planning to support your daughter. The rest of you will have to fend for yourselves."

- Church Building Repairs:
  The minister was preoccupied with thoughts of how he was going to ask the congregation to come up with more money than they were expecting for repairs to the church building. Therefore, he was annoyed to find that the regular organist was sick and a substitute had been brought in at the last minute. The substitute wanted to know what to play. "Here's a copy of the service," he said impatiently. "But you'll have to think of something to play after I make the announcement about the finances." During the service, the minister paused and said, "Brothers and sisters, we are in great difficulty; the roof repairs cost twice as much as we expected, and we need four thousand dollars more. Any of you who can pledge one hundred dollars or more, please stand up."

At that moment, the substitute organist played, "The Star–Spangled Banner!" And that is how the substitute became the regular organist!

- God loves a cheerful giver not a tearful one.

- Christians in a Trance:
  Did you know that many Christians are falling into trances these days? It usually happens about offering time at church.

- Some people hold onto their money so tightly at offering time that even George Washington gets tears in his eyes from the pain.

- After the church service, a little boy told the pastor, "When I grow up, I'm going to give you some money." "Well, thank you," the pastor replied. "But why?" "Because my daddy says you're one of the poorest preachers we've ever had."

- Three boys are in the schoolyard bragging about their fathers. The first boy says, "My dad scribbles a few words on a piece of paper, he calls it a poem, they give him one hundred dollars." The second boy says, "That's nothing. My dad scribbles a few words on a piece of paper, calls it a prescription, and they give him five hundred dollars." The third boy says, "I got you both beat. My dad scribbles a few words on a piece of paper, he calls it a sermon, and it takes twelve people to collect all the money!"

- Tithing Pays!

Two men crashed in their private plane on a South Pacific island. Both survived.

One of the men brushed himself off and then proceeded to run all over the island to see if they had any chance of survival. When he returned, he rushed up to the other man and screamed, "This Island is uninhabited; there is no food; there is no water. We are going to die!"

The other man leaned back against the fuse-lage of the wrecked plane, folded his arms, and responded, "No we're not. I make over 250,000 dollars a week."

The first man grabbed his friend and shook him. "Listen, we are on an uninhabited island. There is no food, no water. We are going to die!"

The other man, unruffled, again responded. "No, I make over 250,000 dollars a week."

Mystified, the first man, taken aback with such an answer again repeated, "For the last time, I'm telling you we are doomed. There is no one else on this island. There is no food. There is no water. We are, I repeat, we are going to die a slow death."

Still unfazed, the first man looked the other in the eyes and said, "Do not make me say this again. I make over 250,000 dollars per week. I tithe. My pastor will find us!"

- "The safest way to double your money is to fold it over and put it in your pocket." Ken Hubbard.